The Stro'

The Str

Published by

Percychatteybooks Publishing

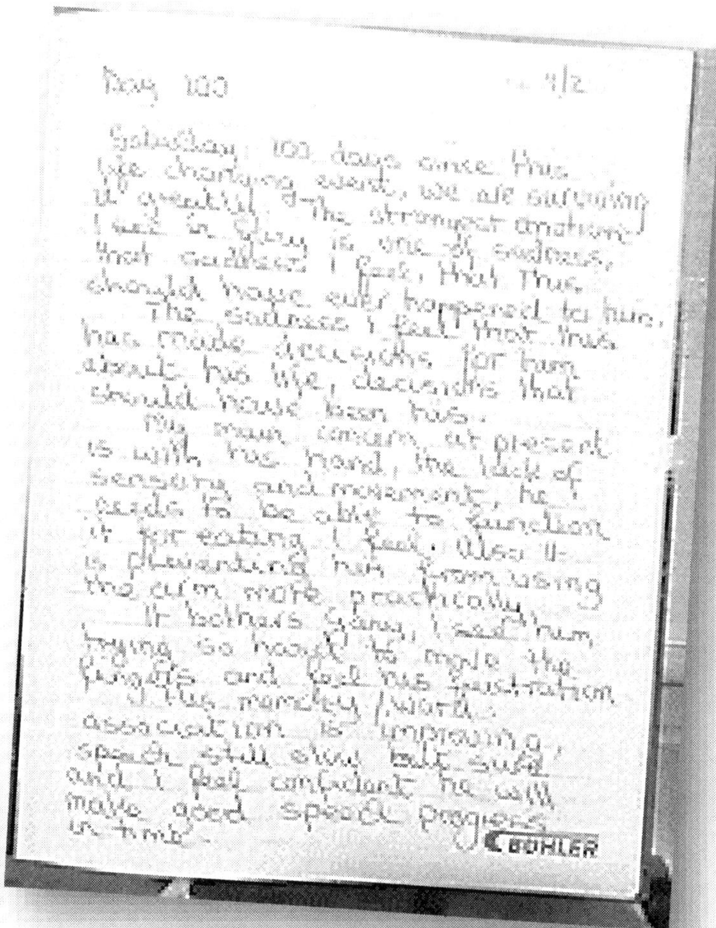

Day 100 4/2

Saturday 100 days since this life changing event, we are surviving it greatfully. The strongest emotion I feel in Gary is one of sadness, that sadness I feel, that this should have ever happened to him.
The sadness I feel that this has made decisions for him about his life, decisions that should have been his.
My main concern at present is with his hand, the lack of sensing and movement he needs to be able to function it for eating I feel. Also it is preventing him from using the arm more practically.
It bothers Gary, I see him trying so hard to move the fingers and feel his frustration.
His memory / word association is improving, speech still slow but sure and I feel confident he will make good speech progress in time.

A page of the day to day diary as kept by the Author

The Stroke

The Diaries of

OUR EXTRAORDINARY JOURNEY

Pauline Yates

Acknowledgments

My first thank you goes to my amazing Husband, who has been not only my best friend throughout this journey, but he has also lent his support to me against all the odds. He has taught me humility and gratitude, when I felt neither, and he has shown me, that when you are on the scariest ride of your life, it is so much less terrifying, when you are sitting next to the person you most trust with your life.

Gary you are my hero and I bow to your superior charm at all times. You are the most perfect and complete Human being I know.

My never-ending thank you, goes to The Zilschlacht Rehab Clinic in Switzerland and its staff, where they made us safe and welcome, taught us skills, allowed me to be an integral part of life there, and gave us the confidence to learn, and move forward on our own.

Also, to Patrik and Stephanie from Therapiezentrum Schritt Fur Schritt in St Gallen Switzerland, who welcomed Gary as an outpatient to their small private practice and further progressed his skills, Stephanie for her positivity and Patrik for his enthusiasm.

Our final Clinic thank you, goes to the Ambulantereha Clinic in St Gallen and the Therapists who continue to support Gary and check on his recovery.

To my publisher Percy Chattey, for all the help and advice, and the encouraging words along the way, without him this book would have remained on my Laptop.

So many people have joined us on this journey, too many to thank individually, but I am nothing if not certain that you all know who you are. Each and every-one of you, is important to us, your constant love and encouragement lifts our spirits on a daily basis.

It is with hope in our hearts, that we can rely on your support, for the next leg of this incredible journey.

We have little idea of where it will continue to take us, or how long we will need to reach the summit, but we look forward to seeing everyone at the top.

Gary

THIS BOOK IS DEDICATED TO MY HUSBAND
AND ANYONE ELSE WHO IS A STROKE SURVIVOR ON
THEIR OWN JOURNEY

Pauline Yates

The Stroke

OUR EXTRAORDINARY JOURNEY

This remarkable story recorded diligently as it happened, depicting when the life as the couple knew it, without warning, came to a sudden end.

Written by Pauline Yates, who clearly explains the horror, the difficulties and struggles when her husband's way of living, with no pre-indication, is abruptly ended.

A shocking true account of a female pouring out her true love to a life partner, in an attempt to bring him out of the darkness that has blighted his mind, so they can resume some form of living together, although very different from which was previously theirs

This will bring tears to your eyes - it did mine : editor

The Stroke

OUR EXTRAORDINARY JOURNEY

Pauline Yates

DAY ONE

Friday 2nd November 2018 16.00 hours

Location: Benidorm, Spain

Funny, not Ha-ha, but more satirical really, how that particular second in life manifests itself without warning.

One second you think you have it all, love, life, happiness, hopes and plans for the future, a cold beer and tapas on the table in front of you, relaxed and looking forward to spending a fun filled few days together.

'BANG'

In a flash, in a heartbeat our World tilts then turns upside down, will we cling on?

The day our World changed forever, was when my husband Gary had a severe Ischemic Stroke at the age of 56.

We were chatting normally, I turned to look out of the window, when suddenly the table shook and the drinks nearly fell, I turned to see what my husband was doing, and there it was, a full- blown stroke in progress.

The Bar is noisy. I am shouting for help. Gary is struggling to stay conscious.

I am struggling to hold him on the chair, he has no control of anything. He is drooling. His mouth is lopsided.

He's drawing away from our World, the stroke is obvious, all the symptoms are there, and seem magnified. I am in a mad panic. I shout, "*Ambulance, Ambulance, he's having a stroke*". Two strangers are holding him up now, they want to lay him on the floor, I say no, I must keep him conscious, I keep talking to him, look at me, don't close your eyes, stay with me I say.

My heart is beating so fast I can feel the pulse in my head. Where is the ambulance? I am desperate for someone to help, I stare into his eyes, willing him to stay with me, he can see me, I keep talking to him, I ask him to say my name, his mouth does not work, I won't let go, I know he will be desperately trying to stay with me. Gary has that terrible indescribable fear in his eyes, the same fear I have in my heart, a fear you can only understand if you have experienced it, a fear that they are slipping away from you, and you are powerless to bring them back. I must not let him go.

I keep repeating in my head, he's having a stroke, I can't seem to stop it, we need help, we need help right now, I want to scream, but I am already shouting for help, what else can I do. Everyone is looking at us. Suddenly, the bar seems quiet, no one is talking, just staring.

Everyone looks very sorry for us. They all understand what is going on. But it's not happening to them, it's happening to us. It's happening to my husband, how can this be?

GARY

My husband, and soulmate, a charismatic, charming, witty and funny, highly intelligent guy, the kind you can always rely on. Aged just 56 at the time of his stroke. No medical conditions, not overweight, healthy and fit lifestyle. Based in Switzerland working for a Swiss Company, extremely experienced at his job role, highly respected by everyone he worked with, loved by all his family and friends. We have a great marriage and lifestyle, he is my best friend for sure, both working hard at our respective careers, living between Spain, where we have a beautiful home, and a plan to retire there one day, and Switzerland, enjoying everything both Countries have to offer. Skiing weekends and holidays during the winter Season, riding our motorbikes in Spain during the Summer, and enjoying an amazing social life with friends there.

Gary is a natural sportsman and he was a good golfer. He loves every aspect of skiing, particularly the Après ski.

We went to Ibiza for a week every year, where we loved the music, the dancing and the chilled atmosphere, relaxing all day in the

sunshine, enjoying the sangria and gin and tonics and staying out till the early hours enjoying the vibe from the young ones.

Gary is the sort of person who loves to make people laugh, he is brilliant at laughing at himself, and he is also brilliant at telling a funny story. He will go the extra mile just to make you laugh.

He is the most honest person I know, incapable of telling a lie, he is extremely loyal, but if you do not return his loyalty he will happily walk away.

His loyalty extended to a thirty two year career at Rolls Royce Aerospace, where at the age of forty nine he decided he had no further promotion prospects, so he took the massive step of seeking a position with another Company.

Gary moved to London to work with a Swiss Company for two years, then he was invited to make the move to Switzerland and join the team there. He had reached the pinnacle of his career and was at the peak of his earning power, but more importantly, he loved his job and envisaged many more years at it.

Gary travelled globally within his role, and had a very responsible position within the Company, I have been asked many times if I thought stress played a big part in his stroke, but I have to say, that Gary is not a person to stress about things, he has a very calm and calming personality, also, he was so experienced in his work that he never showed any signs of stress.

My ultimate answer to this question is, and I have said it before, that after the event it is no good trying to look for an answer, reason or excuse, or looking to blame anything or any-one, it is what it is, accepting it has happened is the only answer.

There were no signs leading up to the stroke, in one second, this life, our life, came to an abrupt end, no warning, no preparation, no second chance and no turning the clock back.

An unthinkable reality had entered our World, and would instantly take over our lives, and change them forever, whether we liked it or not.

However, we had no idea what a tough journey we were about to embark on, we were to take an adventure that we could never dream we would be taking. I knew we were facing a mountain ahead, one that we would have to climb inch by inch to reach the top, to be able to see the view that we could no longer see, but I had no idea how long it would take.

Our Journey Begins

Sirens in the distance, silence in my head, everything happening around me. My heart is thumping. I feel feint, I have to concentrate, it's hard to think straight, its true what they say, everything goes in slow motion at a time like this. Everyone is staring, but no one knows what to do, it's just like being frozen in time, the sirens get louder.

"He's going to be ok, is he going to be ok? "

The Paramedics arrive, they are slow, too slow, their arrival shows no sense of urgency. I think maybe they assume he is drunk because he is slumped in a bar in Benidorm, such as its reputation is these days. I have to tell them, but I don't know the word for Stroke in Spanish. I pull one Paramedic over and point to Gary's face, yes, yes, he sees now what is happening, he understands.

They soon place him on a stretcher and take him outside to the ambulance. I have to wait on the street, they are working on him for 20 minutes, it feels more like two hours. I am sweating with stress, I can't think straight, no one is with me, I pace up and down, struggling to stay calm. I see people watching from the bar, people passing by and looking at me, I feel totally detached from any form of reality in my head, and yes, I am frightened beyond belief.

Finally, we are driving away, I am in the front passenger seat next to the driver. I am desperate to be with Gary, but they won't let me. I can't see him, I suddenly have a panic attack, fears that he is dead, I can't breathe properly, I can't talk, I actually feel like I am having a heart attack, I think how bizarre that would be, then I think how bizarre it is to be thinking that!

I assume we are going to a Hospital in Benidorm, so should be there very fast, soon I realise we are heading for the motorway, surely we are not going to Alicante, but maybe it's the best Emergency room.

There are no sirens, I think this is strange as the traffic is heavy and he stops at traffic lights and roundabouts, I am frantic, I indicate about the traffic, but he ignores me.

Just before the motorway, we pull over, I ask what is happening, again he just ignores me, he leaves the ambulance and by the time I get out they are taking Gary out on the stretcher, I am completely confused now, I ask what is going on, one of them tells me an Ambulance is coming from Alicante to transport us the rest of the way.

Am I hearing correct, this is a stroke victim, everyone knows that time is the most important thing, the faster they get help the more you save of them, that's what we see on the Public information adverts isn't it? I have seen plenty of them. I am at Gary's side now, trying my best to reassure him, but I don't think he hears me, he is barely conscious, I feel like screaming at the Paramedics, I feel I am going mad. Maybe ten minutes later the other Ambulance arrives, and he is transferred.

Another forty five minutes' drive to Alicante Hospital, so much traffic on the motorway, an unbearable panic is setting in, if I could see him, reassure him , I know I would feel better, the driver is talking to me, I am looking at him but can't take in what he is saying, I just stare vacantly at him. He keeps talking, I suppose that's what they do, try to distract you, well it isn't working, all I can think about is that my lovely husband has had a stroke, I keep trying to tell myself that he will be ok, he is a fighter, he is strong, he wouldn't leave me like this.

The journey on the motorway is agonising, it's very busy, the driver is cross because some cars don't get out of his way even with the lights and sirens wailing. I think what a stressful job this is, yet he's not had a stroke, I think about some of the really stressful times I have had, yet I didn't have a stroke. Useless thoughts that don't mean anything and don't achieve anything, but I can't control them, my mind is just racing.

We are at Emergency in Alicante now, everything happening very fast, I just follow behind, they place him in a bay and close the curtains around him, there is no seat so I stand and hold his hand, nurses come and check him over, they ask him questions but he is non responsive, they ask me what happened, how long ago, his name, his date of birth, I can hardly remember my own name at this point let alone all these questions.

I need to pull myself together, clear my head of this fog. Suddenly they are taking Gary away, they tell me to follow, then they disappear. I am alone suddenly, no one is here, a silent corridor, my thoughts come rushing in all at once, like a tidal wave crashing through my head, my whole nervous system is jingling, he wasn't conscious I realise, but he was alive, not struggling anymore, he was on oxygen, that's good I tell myself. I sit on the only chair there and I have to close my eyes and shut out all this white.

Someone appears, I have to sign papers, they explain that he has had a very severe Ischemic Stroke, they have to remove the clot, he needs surgery, I have to sign a consent form, they say he will not survive if they don't operate immediately.

I sign the form and she disappears, leaving me alone in a white sterile corridor, sitting on a hard chair, nothing to look at, nothing to occupy my thoughts.

I start to think about the car being in Benidorm, how will I get it back, our weekend cases are at the hotel, should I call the hotel. I suddenly remember I had bought some clothes before we went to lunch and I had left the bags on the floor in the bar, I had not paid the bill for the food or drink, would the hotel reception wonder why we did not come back. Ridiculous thoughts are crowding my mind.

Two hours turns into three hours, it feels like ten, it feels like a lifetime waiting, will it be forever? Will he come back to me?
Tick Tock Tick Tock

They appear with Gary, I stand automatically, I feel like I want to pass out, but of course I take a deep breath and prepare myself. He's back, looks peaceful, just Gary sleeping, no signs of anything untoward, no hint of medical intervention, he looks normal somehow, my spirits soar, he's back with me. He needs to sleep. I will watch over him.

The nurse is talking, saying something about intensive care, the Doctor will come to see me, follow them, so I do, holding Gary's hand, it's very warm but so is mine, I am here Gary, I am not going anywhere.

It is so quiet here in intensive care, sterile and white, glass boxes with someone very poorly in each box, everyone linked to drips and machines supporting them, ensuring that life goes on, Gary will be the same.

Sound only in my head, the quiet is deafening, the silence disturbing, no movement, only from the nurse. Fear gripping me, I need to take a deep breath, stop my heart from beating so fast, fear is rising.

This can't really be happening to us, it is happening, it's happened. I have realisation that he has actually had a stroke, it's a bad stroke, not a mini stroke, a severe stroke, this will change our lives from this point on.

I feel tears stinging my eyes, I close them and silently talk to myself, he needs me to find my inner most strength from here on in, I feel a hand on my arm, a nurse asking me in Spanish if I am alright, I nod my head and smile to reassure her I am ok, but I am not ok, I feel lost, frightened, useless to assess the situation, it's too soon to assess things.

What time is it? How much time has passed? I don't know, I have no concept of time now, I think it is evening, maybe night, what do I do now? I can't leave him; I won't leave him I need to stay close.

I need to be here, he needs to see me when he wakes up, I notice now that there is no one else with the other patients in any of the other glass boxes, no family at the bedsides, at that moment I make my mind up I will not leave if they ask me to, and I have no car, I suddenly remember again my car is in Benidorm, our cases, I must contact the hotel, my mind goes blank I can't remember the name of the hotel, of course I have that in my phone, I don't know how I will speak to them on the phone and explain without breaking down, my emotions are so near to the surface.

Realisation hits me like a sledgehammer, I have to contact Gary's Parents, and the family, to tell them what has happened, dread fills me for the task ahead, how to break the news from afar, I think about how far away everyone is and how impossible for anyone to help me. I think about his father, he's a strong individual, calm, he will be able to deal with it, explain it to his mother.

DAY TWO

Alicante Hospital: Intensive Care Unit.

The night was agonisingly long and uncomfortable, sitting on a chair, its climate controlled in this sterile box, I have nothing but the clothes I came in, I'm so cold, no one offers me a blanket or a drink, there is just a night nurse sitting silently at her station, she is not interested in me, no interaction, no concern for me, I'm not her problem and I chose to stay here.

Gary has not moved, he looks peaceful, is that good or worrying, I don't know which, I check my emotions, no use for overreaction , that's just dangerous and not pro-active, I hate the World suddenly, terrible thoughts trying to infiltrate my mind, I need to focus more.

The door opens, a Doctor in a white coat, stereotypical smile on his face like we are just about to have a sociable chat. I smile back at him whilst stiffly standing up, we shake hands as he introduces himself, I instantly forget his name, please, sit down he says, so I obey.

Your husband has suffered a clot on his brain, the procedure to remove it was a success, the artery is clear and open, I let out my breath, my spirit soars instantly, he's going to be alright. Then I hear words like, paralysis, right side, leg, arm, instantly things start springing into my head, like I have already been planning for it, driving, skiing, motorbike, golf, quickly followed by, dressing, work, Life.

The Stroke

Can he hear the Doctor? Does he understand what they are saying? Does he know what is happening right now? I don't know the answer to these questions, how can I, do I understand? Oh yes, I understand perfectly, this is a situation, a very serious situation, and it has to be faced very quickly by me, he needs me to be strong, positive and reassuring. There is not going to be an easy solution to this.

I feel isolated, kind of funny really when I have no time on my own, I'm isolated in a crowded room, almost like being at a party where you don't know anyone and no one takes any notice of you, you want to talk to someone but they are not looking at you.

I'm thinking, this is not about me, this is actually about Gary, then I accept, that yes, this is about me also, this is about us, this didn't just happen to him, it also happened to me, this will turn my life upside down the same. Now is the perfect time to find my inner and outer strength, he will need me to hold him physically and emotionally, I know I have that strength, I have needed it before and now he needs it.

Spending all night on a chair fully clothed is not a strength builder for sure, it is however, a time for thoughts and plans to form. One day at a time they say, and its good advice, but certain situations call for longer term plans, I have so much to organise, so many people to call, I need to get some of this stuff out of my head. Time to break the news whilst he is still asleep, parents, family then work, in that order.

I need everyone to be strong also, I can't prop anyone up, not even Gary's parents, I feel so bad having to bring this news to them. I know how they will feel not being able to come and see him, but I can't change that. Once the calls are made, I won't have to do that job again, I need to do this calmly, take the emotion out of it, and just give them the basic details for now. I need to contact his Medical Insurance; they will need to take over the official side for me.

I will have so many decisions to make on his behalf, they will be experienced at all this, they will guide me through these first days. Will he be able to travel to Switzerland? I feel a burning desire to take him to Switzerland, every fibre of my being says it will be better for him.

On the negative side, we have no friends or family there to support us, but I still feel it will be better. I need to talk to his Medical Insurance to see what they think, I need to find out if they will repatriate him, they need to be involved and advise me of what options he has with them. I am faced with two foreign Countries, neither of which I speak the language sufficiently enough to communicate properly on such a level. The UK is not an option for me, I have seen how people in the UK are treated after a stroke, there is very little support system in place, so that is not even on the list.

My inner most thoughts are dangerously near the surface, he's not going to be happy about this, of course he's not going to be happy, he's had a serious stroke at 56 years of age, in his prime, at the peak of his career, his World has been turned upside down, his future plans cut short, thrown off his path, no of course he won't be happy, who could blame him.

Suddenly I think "Adventure", the word literally just popped into my head, I realise I have been catapulted into another dimension, another facet of life as I know it, so we just go on an adventure, to a place that we never thought we would go to, isn't life just one big adventure, one way or another?

We will take a new path, holding each other's hands, and supporting each other, sometimes it will be scary I'm certain, but that's when we will hold on tighter to each other.

There is no path to go back now, the door has been closed and cannot be reopened, not ever, so we must take the many paths that lay beyond our knowledge at this moment in time, but we will gain knowledge on the way. Paths much harder for Gary than me, some will have stones and boulders he must climb, some will be slippery and hard for him to balance, but what he will have, is me by his side to support and encourage him, step by step we will make our journey together.

I need to stay focused, it's difficult, my mind keeps wandering, too much time sitting in this chair, no one to talk to, waiting all the time for Gary to wake, waiting for the Doctor, I need an update, if there is one, I need food and drink, I haven't eaten since this happened, I am still wearing the same clothes, I haven't showered, no one cares.

Shouldn't someone here care about me, after all, I am the only person he has here, don't they want me to be able to cope. Am I feeling sorry for myself? Yes, I am, I feel no guilt, I am only human, after all.

**

s looming to the surface, anxiety, stress, tension, my head is full of cotton wool, I need to start plans today, I need to make those phone calls, so much to do. I need some control over the situation.

I am surprised at how calmly I dealt with the call to the Hotel and even Gary's Parents, his Father was, as I expected, calm, supportive and understanding of my need to keep it short.

Next the call to Gary's Company in Switzerland, once this is done, it's time for me to get this terrible news out there for everyone, I take the easy option and post a status on Facebook.

I speak to the Insurance Company and they reassure me that the best option is Switzerland for Gary's rehabilitation, they will take control of this, they will speak with the Doctors and get an update, it feels good to have someone who is used to such situations taking over important aspects. The guy is nice, he asks about me, the first person who sounds genuinely concerned about me, he tells me to make sure I am eating and getting sleep, reassures me that they will do everything to help, he will call me back after he has spoken to the Doctor.

I need to eat, I don't feel hungry but I know it's stupid not to, I go back into Gary, he looks peaceful, I speak to the nurse tell her I will be in the canteen and will be back very soon, she just nods, no interaction.

The canteen has worse than typical hospital food, a non-event, I couldn't swallow anything, just a coffee. On one side it's full of worried looking people, maybe families waiting for news of loved ones, also sick looking people. On the other side are doctors and nurses, eating, chatting, smiling and oblivious to us. I need to get back to Gary. The Doctor is coming to give me an update I don't want to miss him.

The Doctor arrives, the same one as yesterday, he explains that Gary was placed in an induced coma after the operation, they will bring him out of it tomorrow.

I ask if he will be ok, then wonder why I am asking such a stupid question, of course they don't know the answer till they try it, he is kind, he explains this to me. If everything goes to plan, they will take him for a brain scan and should have more information for me then. I tell him I need to go and sort the car out, he tells me to do it today, and to go home for some rest then come back tomorrow, of course I know I am not going to do that, so I just nod my head.

The Stroke

It's time for me to enlist help, I call our friend Alan, of course he's shocked and upset at the news, but supportive and agrees to drive me to Benidorm to pick the car up, and I will go to the bar to get my bags.

It's good to have someone to talk to, someone to say everything is going to be alright, I know it probably isn't going to be for a long time but it's nice to hear it. I remember looking out of the window and thinking, it's a beautiful day, I am on my way to Benidorm and poor Gary is stuck in that glass box, strange thoughts.

Alan drops me outside the Bar, it is very quiet when I walk in, it's a bit surreal being back here so soon, I feel a strange detached feeling. I instantly want to get out of the bar, the barman recognises me, doesn't speak just gets the bags, and hands me the bill for the food and drink we had, 28 Euro. I think how lucky it is I brought my purse, then think how awful it is to present the bill to me, I pay it and leave, he didn't even ask how Gary was, it didn't bother me as I didn't want to talk anyway.

At the hotel I explain the situation, the Receptionist just looks at me with no expression, she then prints off a bill, a 2-night stay including car park fee for 2 days, although we didn't actually use the room.

Again, I feel very detached, people wandering around the lobby, sitting by the pool drinking cocktails, doing things we should be doing at this very moment, at this very location.

Sadness swoops over me, I need to get out of here, I suddenly feel that these people just have no idea what is going on in my life, and seriously they don't care. I need to get back to the hospital, not looking forward to the drive, I need to stay calm, no speeding, I need to be able to concentrate, that's a difficult thing at the moment, my mind wanders about of its own free will, darting about in confusion most of the time. It's just too difficult to control my thoughts at present.

It's funny, how minutes separate each other in your mind, stay with me here, one minute your thinking about where to go at the next roundabout to get onto the motorway, the next your wondering how you got to Alicante so quick, we have all been there, on a journey that you barely remember driving the route, but arrived safely.

Walking back to the ward I think about Switzerland, I wish the Insurance guy would call, just at that moment, like thought transference, my phone rings and it's him.

The Stroke

He is so nice, very reassuring, he has a very calming voice and manner, but of course this is his job, these people are used to dealing with tragedy and emotional people, he tells me he has been updated with Gary's situation, and assures me that the best course of action is repatriation to Switzerland. I am assured that Gary will not get the same help in Spain as he will in Switzerland, deep down I know he is correct. The time is not right yet as Gary is not stable enough to move, but as soon as he is out of intensive care he will go into a private ward. Once he is well enough, we will be flown back. He tells me that he will be kept updated by the Doctor and will be in touch with me at every stage, and if I need anything, I am to call him, He also tells me that I will always speak to him so will not have to explain things again to anyone, I feel a massive weight lifted, I know someone is fighting in my corner now. Every fibre in my body tells me that we are making the right decision for Gary's long -term recovery.

I make my way back to Gary, I talk to him, telling him the plan so far, and hoping my voice is reassuring to him, I tell him he is safe and that tomorrow he will be awake, and I will be here. I chat to him about what I have been doing, how Alan helped me and tell him that I am fine, and that things are sorting out. I have no idea whether he can hear me.

My phone beeps, its Artur, Gary's colleague from work and our friend, I dread answering the phone, but go to the corridor and do so, I don't want to cry, but I feel the sting of tears in my eyes, I didn't have time to prepare for this conversation and I don't want to upset him along with myself.

The call is a bit of a blur, but he says he is flying over, he needs to see Gary, that's all I remembered of the conversation, apart from he said he will call again later when he has made plans.

I suddenly realise how upset people will be, a stroke is not like an illness where you have time to prepare along the way, no, a stroke is so sudden that it takes time to adjust to what's happened, the news will still be filtering through to people, I have had to text a few people as I can't face talking to them on the phone, but news will still be travelling, via Facebook and word and mouth. I can't speak to everyone yet.

So much to think about now, I need to get back to the house, I need to pack things to take with us as I don't know how long it will be before we return to Spain, I need to sort the house out, close it up, where will I leave the car, what clothes should I take, then I think to myself, it's all crap really, I don't really care about all that stuff, its energy wasting emotion, who cares, I just need to secure the house and car then leave it.

A calm swoops in, I feel like laughing at myself, I don't know why, but I think it is because I really don't care, I just want to get the Swiss trip organised as soon as possible. I have to face facts though, I have no time scale to run to, Gary has to be fit to fly before it happens. How long will he be in intensive care, then he has to go to recovery, I should know more when I see the Doctor again.

Tomorrow Artur will arrive, I am so grateful for his support, he is another one of my hero's of the moment, he made a decision to come no matter what anyone else advised, this decision could have been at the risk of his job, but he told me he was coming no matter what.

This decision will be one that I will never forget, my gratitude will last as long as I live. This young man has more integrity and loyalty than a lot of people, he has become family to us, it has been uplifting for me today. I tell Gary the news from Artur. I told him I needed someone to help me, that Artur would be bringing documents from our flat, documents that I will need once we arrive back in Switzerland. I am still not even sure how much Gary understands when I talk to him, there is no flicker from his eyes, no response, but I am comforted to be talking to him.

DAY THREE

It's like I have fallen into a fast-flowing stream,
It's pulling me forward, but I am not going under.
The flow is fast and strong, clinging to my clothes.
At first my instincts tell me to turn and swim back.
But, it's too powerful, I can't swim against the flow.
It's Inevitable that I will be swept away, feeling helpless.
It's safer to let the flow take me, until I reach a safe point

Gary is awake, no complications thank goodness, but my heart is breaking, he can't talk, he has a tube feeding him. He is looking at me, such fear in his eyes, does he realise what's happened I just don't know, should I tell him yet, I just don't know. I have to wait for the Doctor, hopefully he will help me.

The smiling Doctor arrives, we shake hands again, here goes, I have a thousand questions and I am looking for answers to them all. I don't have a chance to ask one, he tells me they are taking Gary for a scan to see what injury has been sustained. Another agonising wait.

The nurse tells me to go to the canteen to have some food and a drink, she will send someone to fetch me when Gary is back, I think they just need me out of the way.

My friend Tricia, a very new friend here in Spain called, it's very difficult speaking to her without being too emotional, I don't want to break down, it's so very hard to take control again, I need my strength for more positive things, she insists that she will come to the hospital to have a coffee with me, I don't think I can face it but I say yes, I can feel that she wants to see me, she says even for just 10 minutes, to be able to give me a hug.

I am not sure now, on looking back, what I must have looked like at this time, the same clothes for 3 days, no makeup, no hair done, a chair to try to sleep on at night, it's funny how it doesn't have a place in your mind at the time.

I feel happier in the canteen this time, he's awake and we will get more information today, my spirits are lifting, he looks poorly of course, and the tubes and equipment don't help, but I look past all that, but he looks like Gary, even his face has lifted it does not look paralysed on one side, in fact I can't remember which side it was now, that seems strange, I visualise the time of the stroke, try to remember which side he couldn't move his arm, which side his mouth dropped, which stroke the Doctor said he had, how bizarre I can't remember.

It was nice to see a friendly face, share a coffee with Tricia, I feel a mess, I don't even feel clean, but she does not looked surprised or shocked, I know she is holding that all in for my sake, I give her the news I have so far, but she does not press me further, I try to hide my jingling nerves, but I know she sees them. She is so calm, so supportive, telling me to look after myself, that Gary needs me fit and healthy. I realise how lucky I am to have her in our lives, and grateful for this little visit.

The Stroke

I make my way back to ICU, it is the putting a smile on my face that is so hard, he looks so sad, I see it in his eyes, I go to him and take his hand, he cries silently, huge tears roll down his face, I move in and take him in my arms, I can feel the tears wet on my cheek, I am desperate to let my tears fall but I have to hold them back. This is not the time for me to cry, I am sure the time will come, but not now.

A nurse comes to take me to see the Doctor, I hate leaving him now he's awake, I tell him where I am going and not to worry, he's alive and awake and we will be ok, it seems so little to offer him, but I don't have anything else yet.

The news is devastating, confirmation that he has a severe injury to the left side of the brain, resulting in paralysis down the right side of his body, he can't move his arm or leg, he has no sensory in them either, throat paralysis, can't swallow, no peripheral vision, so can't see either side of him, no control of his bowel or urinary tract, due to a massive infection, common with a stroke apparently, causing total incontinence, and finally, he has lost his speech, it's highly unlikely that he will walk again.

I feel suddenly overwhelmed, I'm drowning, being pulled down into a black hole, I feel sick in my stomach, my head is hurting, I stand up, I sit down, I don't want to be there, I want to be anywhere but there, my hands start to shake, the Doctor asks if I am alright, I say yes!

Gary will be moved to a private room tomorrow where he will be monitored and looked after, until we are fit to go to Switzerland. I need to get back to him, I need to reassure him, we will get through this, we are strong, I am strong and I have determination, I am not a quitter and neither is he, I take a deep breath, try to slow my heartbeat, whatever the future holds, we will not be letting go, we will not be victims in this, that is for other people not us. I will be with him every step of this journey, supporting, encouraging, I have no room for weak emotions taking over where strong emotions will prevail.

I must leave him to go and get him some pyjamas, the thought fills me with dread, I don't know where to go, but go I must. I enter the car park and walk to where I thought I left the car, my car is not there, I start to panic, I walk quickly the perimeter of the floor, nothing, I run up the first flight of stairs and run round looking, nothing, a second flight of stairs, the same outcome, no car.

I start to panic, I'm sweating profusely and I have terrible palpitations, I run down repeating my search on each floor, my stress levels are rocketing through the roof, I now feel as though I may have a heart attack. I feel like my coping mechanism is about to snap.

I run to the kiosk and tell the attendant I can't find my car, he asks if I have the ticket, I give it to him, he scans it and tells me it is on the lower level. I never knew they could do this. I am so grateful, I had not realised that the drive in entrance goes down to the underground level, but the pedestrian entry is on the ground level, I missed this completely, so I was unaware that there was a below ground level. Your mind does not work properly in this type of situation, it's so hard to think straight or logically. I say to myself, one day I will laugh at this.

Later I must pick Artur up from the airport, I am not certain how I will deal with seeing him, but so far I have been strong, no tears, I never considered myself a cry baby in difficult situations, and I am strong when dealing with other people's misfortune, although I cry at sad and romantic films.

No one has seen Gary apart from the Hospital staff, I am very nervous about how Artur will deal with seeing Gary in intensive care, he is very fond of him, I have to tell him to be strong, and not show any negative emotions, no tears. It's important for Gary to see hope in people's eyes, I know it's a lot to ask, but he will understand, and I know he will be strong for Gary.

When will that safe point be? I feel sure that I will know when the time is right, I will recognise when it's safe to stand up, when I know I will no longer be swept along, when I can safely take Gary with me, to carry on our life together, with no intervention, but for now, I just need to keep us both safe.

Artur's visit is here, it has to be short, Gary will be moved this evening, I tell Gary that Artur is here, he tries desperately to smile, I feel his pain, I know he does not really want Artur to see him like this, he will be feeling vulnerable, of course he will, but it's important for Artur and also for me, someone else needs to know the seriousness of what is happening, I need someone else who understands where we are, and someone I trust to pass on the news.

As soon as Artur sees Gary from outside the glass box, I see huge watery bubbles cover his eyes, I look towards him, begging him not to break down, he smiles a very nervous but big smile, brushing away his tears and recovering himself the best he can, I look at him and think how young he is to be dealing with this, my gratitude is immense at this moment, I feel that it is he who needs a hug of reassurance.

Artur's visit is very short, he looks tired and I am also concerned about him, he leaves for his hotel and I hope he gets a good night's sleep, we will see him again tomorrow. Everything seems to move so fast all the time.

Tomorrow we will be moved to a different room, no glass box, no sick people in our eyeline, I will get a different chair to spend my nights on, no doubt.

The night is so long, too much silent time, Gary sleeps fitfully, not the sleep of peace, tears fall all the time, he doesn't move, only his head to look at me, I lay beside him on the bed, I really don't care if it's not permitted, but the nurse isn't interested, she would only react if any of his buzzers sound.

I find myself wondering if they actually think of any of these patients as people, they seem to be so detached, there is no bedside manner, no caring façade that I can sense, I feel it's strange to be in that career if you have no empathy towards these people, she's maybe, in her thirties, old enough to understand yet not old enough to be blasé about life surely. I think how desperate it must be for people who are sick but have no one to fight for them, everyone needs someone to look out for them, but not everyone is lucky enough.

I am cold again, I hate being cold, I look at my hands, they look so white, I have goose-bumps, on my arms, I hold Gary's hand, it is wet with sweat, I touch his forehead he feels very clammy, I speak to him but he does not respond, suddenly I feel a fear, my instinct tells me something is different, something has changed, something does not feel right.

What time is it, it's the middle of the night, he seems too calm, I start to panic, I go to the nurse and tell her I think something is wrong, she doesn't understand, I beckon her to come with me, she does, I touch his forehead, there are beads of sweat, she does the same.

She goes to get a thermometer; she checks him then she indicates for me to wait and disappears. Soon a female doctor arrives, she smiles but does not speak, she checks his temperature again, then leaves, I have no idea what this means.

Very shortly a porter arrives and they are taking him away, a nurse arrives who speaks English, she tells me they are taking him for a brain scan, I ask why, she says because he has a high temperature, I ask what this means and she say's let's wait till we have scan results. I am lost, I don't know what to think, he's gone, and I am left alone with my thoughts, it's unbearable, I put my head in my hands, close my eyes and try to control the screaming in my head.

I get up and walk to the corridor, who can I call, I can't call anyone it's the middle of the night, and I don't think I could speak if I did call anyone, I walk and walk along the corridors, up and down, pacing, clenching my fists. I feel a sense of anger, what is going on, isn't there enough happening right now. I have a real sense of foreboding, again I think, why is this happening, he is supposed to be getting better, he is supposed to be stable. Walking, walking, I can't stay still, can't sit down, looking at the door, willing them to bring him back.

To this day I have no concept of how long they were gone, really, it could have been half an hour or five hours, but they come back, he is not awake. I follow them back into the glass box, I am told the doctor is coming, I know better than to question the nurse, so I just stand at the door and watch, they are replacing the tubes and machines, I notice that they are connecting another drip feed and bag, more fluids, but I don't know what they are.

I hear someone saying my name, I look up and realise I didn't see the doctor arrive, she tells me to sit down, I feel a dread overtaking me, I try to stay calm. She is not smiling, she is being very professional, I just know it's not good news.

Your husband has developed a brain fever she is saying, I look at her and just manage to say yes, nothing else, just yes. We have put him back into a light coma again. I manage to ask, what does this mean, I hear her say, “the next twenty-four hours will tell”, what does that mean, will he be brought round in twenty-four hours, are they just resting his brain.

I have no idea what to think, so I ask her, how did this happen? But there is no answer other than it can happen. She tells me I can stay with him; she doesn’t know I am always with him, but it makes me feel very fearful, I know he is in danger for sure, no-one has said that to me till now. Is this preparing me for the worse. Should I prepare myself for the worse, no, I will not go down that route, he has to get better, he’s not ready to leave yet, not now, not for a long time, it would break too many people’s hearts. He’s a fighter, he can fight this.

The doctor leaves, shaking my hand and telling me that she will pop in first thing in the morning before her shift ends, I thank her. I watch her leave, watching to see if she will look back but of course she doesn’t.

The nurse is talking to me now, asking me if I would like a drink, she thinks he is going to die, that’s what I think to myself, they haven’t bothered with me before, she is trying to be nice, to be sympathetic suddenly, I say yes please, mostly because I don’t know what else to say and I hope a cup of tea will help, I think how British that is.

I go to Gary and hold his hand, I squeeze it gently, I need to tell him that he can’t go anywhere, he has to come back to me. I tell him to fight, we have a life together, we have so much to do, so many plans to fulfil. I ask him, if you die, what will I do without you? I even tell him not to be selfish, I don’t want him to leave me. We have a life and we need to return to it. I feel a warmth, run through my veins, I swear to this day that something happened between us, something that cannot be explained, like a charge passing between two points, I felt it for real, it made me jump. He is not going to leave me; I feel it so strongly. I lay beside him; I will be here until he wakes again.

I sleep a little, so I am surprised when someone touches my arm, I am not sure where I am for a second, then I feel it again, I turn my head and Gary is looking at me, he is awake. I stand up and stare at him, I ask him if he can hear me, he gently nods his head, I kiss him then call the nurse. She checks his temperature, and his blood pressure, checks his drips, I do not ask her any questions, I know the doctor will come soon. I know it will be alright, I know he is not leaving me.

The Stroke

The doctor is smiling as she enters the glass box, we exchange hello's, she checks his chart and asks him if he is alright, he nods, I am smiling as I know it will be positive news, I have absolutely no stress about it. She explains that his temperature has gone down, the antibiotics are working, and his vital signs are good, she tells me not to worry now, and I don't feel worried at all.

The doctor says they will check on Gary again later, and if everything is still ok, then they will move him out of ICU and into a private room.

One day I will tell Gary about what I felt pass between us, but the time is not right now. I consider that being taken to a place worse than I was already in, has given me the understanding and capability to find gratitude in where we are now, are we better off this morning than we were last night? Yes of course we are, would I turn the clock back to last night? No I wouldn't, turning the clock back is not always a good thing. It is far better to try to accept things and live in this moment, than wish for a time in the past, that can never be achieved.

The morning passes very easily, I pop to the canteen while they are washing Gary, a great calm has descended over me, I feel hungry, and realise I would like something to eat, things are looking up. I can't explain it really, but I no longer feel that he is in danger, yes of course he is still very poorly, but I feel we are still on the journey together.

I have to update his parents and I want to speak to my friend Jackie; I know she will be thinking about us, and worrying, I feel strong enough now to have these conversations. People need to know what is going on, and Jackie can update other friends for us.

I take some time now to check my Facebook page, we have lots of messages of support again and it is heart-warming to find people who we have not known very long really, sending us good wishes, along with our long- term friends and family. People in the UK will feel so helpless, unable to help us, and no point in anyone flying out here whilst Gary is in hospital as I will be here with him, so for now Facebook is our point of contact.

I return to Gary and they have him sitting up slightly, I know he is glad to see me, and I am sure he has no idea how glad I am to see him. We pass a couple of hours easily together, I bring him up to date with my calls to his parents and Jackie, read him some messages.

He is checked over again and the news is good, we will move to a private room within the hour, I am hoping we will be there by the time Artur arrives, he will be surprised I am certain to see Gary sitting up and out of ICU.

We are moved, to a different room with a different chair for my nights of thought and further realisation. No machine's connecting Gary to life, just tubes and drips. He is so very weak, not the strong confident man I know, but a very frightened, uncertain and sad soul, he is very broken, very vulnerable, I can only wonder at what his thoughts are.

DAY FOUR

There is no voice, no sound, yet I hear him.
He cannot ask, but I know what he wants.
I feel what he feels, I see all his emotions.
Don't be afraid little bird, I am here, to lift you up.
To strengthen and straighten your wings.
To help you fly again.

Our move goes ok, not very organised, but I have come to expect this in Spain in all aspects of life, not just the hospital. At least we have privacy and time to get Gary stronger, ready for his journey to Switzerland.

I remind him that Artur will be coming any time now, it's so hard to see that he is upset about this, but I explain to him that Artur is family now and I need his support, also he has flown here especially to see him and does he want me to turn him away, of course he smiles knowingly.

Artur arrives again, he speaks Spanish, so he speaks to the Spanish doctor on my behalf, I need Gary's test result papers, I have questions that I want to ask. His support again is calming for me. We have planned to drive to the house together, I need to close it up, I have no idea when I will be back again.

The Stroke

We have to say our goodbyes to Artur, but I know we will see him again soon in Switzerland, it's so hard to stay calm and not break down, and I am sure it's equally as hard for him, but his visit was such a positive time.

Night-time falls upon us only too soon, full of terrors, there is no sleep for us, he is restless. I see the fear, I feel it, how can I help? I lay beside him on the bed, it is wet, he is upset, his catheter has fallen out, I call a nurse. The bed is changed and so is he, its painful to watch, he can't support himself, he cries silently again, it is breaking my heart, I talk to him, words spilling out, trying to sound normal but nothing is normal now.

The nurse leaves without a word, she looks tired and bored, and everything seems too much trouble for her.

I lay beside him on the bed again, I hold him, talk to him, tell him that whatever this is we will survive, and we will fly again together. His silence is so painful to me, where is his voice, what dangerous place are his thoughts in, how can I reassure him when I don't know where this journey will take us. He sleeps, only short naps, then wakes with fear gripping him, dread filling his heart.

The Insurance Company call, they have good news, they are monitoring Gary's progress and have told the Doctors he will be going to Switzerland as soon as he is well enough to fly, my spirits soar, I need to get him out of here, there is no care here, no help, no physio or advice, there is a serious lack of hygiene, they just monitor him, then leave him to lay there. I decide to exercise him myself, I know it is important to get movement as soon as possible, so I start.

His right side has no movement, and no sensory, but I move his leg, all through the day, any kind of exercise I can think of, flexing and bending, it gives us something to focus on, and passes the time for both of us.

It's hard to explain, but knowing that his brain no longer recognises his limbs, is hard for me to understand, I have started to research this particular stroke, so I have a greater understanding, if I am going to help him I need as much knowledge as I can get.

I have seen other people who have had strokes and partners who just did not have the strength to help, recovery in these people is very slow, partners become resentful, even apportioning blame for their lives changing. Being proactive is the only way for us, I will not let him sit and dwell on the negative, I am too positive by nature for that to happen.

Gary cannot eat, he is fed intravenously, it is horrible for him, uncomfortable, with a tube up his nose and down his throat, at night he finds it hard to even get comfortable with his drips and tubes.

I read the many messages of support for him, from my Facebook page to try to relax him and let him see how much people care, I hope he can get some strength from these. He needs sleep to gain more strength, he has a strenuous time ahead.

I think we both dread the nights, I speak to him about the night terrors that creep under the door when the dark arrives to invade your mind. I tell him you have to fight them, don't let them slide into your mind, but that's easy for me to say, I suffer the night terrors myself, you all know that time when you are so tired that you think you will be able to sleep, then the moment you close your eyes, the terrors arrive. So, when they do, I climb in beside him, hold him tight and try to make him feel safe for now.

I ask him tonight, why can't you sleep? Is it because your mind is overthinking, he nods yes, I ask if he is thinking about his motorbike, again he nods yes and the tears flow, what can I say to make him feel better, he loves riding his bike, it is a big part of our lives, I tell him I know what he's thinking, I know exactly what he is thinking, of course I do, I have the same thoughts, but from a different angle. I won't ride my bike if he can't, and bikes have been a part of my life since I was seventeen, but I accept that is the way now.

He's also thinking about his car, will he ever be able to drive again, he's thinking about Golf, will he ever play again, he's thinking about our life, will we have one again. I speak to him about it, I tell him this is not the time to be thinking too much about such things, difficult I know, but we have no idea at this point what the future holds, and we must have hope in our hearts, no one can tell us how far he can go, we have to be strong in mind to deal with the next step first. We are both in the same boat for different reasons, but we are both paddling in the same direction to reach the same destination, and we can only paddle as fast as Gary can.

Focusing on Gary's pain stops me from focusing on mine, when I think about my perfect husband, now so broken that I'm not sure where we start to mend him, it not like mending just one problem, he has multiple problems to sort, but mend him we will, there is a path forward and no matter how hard and steep it is, I will lead him along it.

It's hard to keep your emotions in check, they loom to the surface unexpectedly at times, anxiety, stress, tension. My mind racing all the time, constant hyper-tension, I feel as though I am racing through my thoughts, can't slow them down, I have too many things to think about, too many people to talk to, and too many decisions to make in a short space of time.

My work, my clients have to be notified, a Generic text is sent telling them I will not be back in the UK for the foreseeable future, I apologise for this, I apologise! Although it isn't anyone's fault. I send a polite text, what else can I send. I know that my career is over, in a flash, a decision is made, not my decision, the only decision.

It is confirmed again, the Insurance Company will fly us back to Switzerland as soon as it is safe for Gary, the doctors will decide today, there will be many tests and checks to confirm whether he is stable enough to make the journey, we will be accompanied by a doctor and a nurse, and flown out in a small private aircraft.

I am convinced that Switzerland will bring so much positive energy to us, I'm certain that the health system will be the best possible and he will receive great rehabilitation, I'm counting on these things and hoping I am right.

Left alone again with my thoughts whilst they take Gary for another scan and further tests, I sit and think about how severely injured Gary is, wondering how fit he has to be to make the journey, he is reliant on his drips, he cannot move or support himself, I want him to be safe but I am desperate to leave here, I have chronic sleep deprivation, I am not eating, I know I have lost a lot of weight, I am starting to worry about staying fit myself, I need my strength, but it's difficult as the food is awful in the canteen, even the coffee is undrinkable.

I realise how much harder it is when you don't have the support of family and friends around you, but at the same time I can't imagine having to put a brave face on and making idle chat to anyone. Until we get to Switzerland, we are too transient, I don't want people to make plans and book flights just in case we have to move suddenly. I feel on high alert today, have I done everything here in readiness to leave, I hope so.

The time slowly passes, I go for a walk outside for some fresh air, it's very hot, I feel a little feint, too hot, so I go inside and enter the canteen for a coffee, I can't drink it, waste of money, it's terrible, they should have more respect and caring for visitors.

Back to the room, he is not there yet, sitting trying to slow my thoughts down, I start thinking about what life will be like over the next few months, then realise, it will be as good as I make it, I'm not one to dwell in self-imposed misery, when something happens that is on the negative scale.

I have no time for victims, of course life always goes on, not always the way you expected or made plans for, but you can give in to self- pity and the blame game, but there is no blame game here, it isn't anyone's fault, it's just the card that life deals sometimes, and as we already know, no one said life would be easy.

Most of us have bumpy rides along the way, some bumpier than others I grant you, some people are blessed and have few problematic times, but generally everyone has times of sadness, need, loneliness, life is never plain sailing really.

I have always believed that what you put in you will get back, and if you give to others less fortunate you will receive it back 10 fold, I think I have been a good person, never hurt anyone knowingly, been honest, sometimes to my detriment, and helped people whenever I could, even total strangers, so at present I am feeling that maybe I got this wrong, those old thoughts start to permeate my mind, why Gary, why us, what did we do to deserve this, I stare out of the window, let my mind go blank for a minute, then re-boot and realise, only martyrs ask such questions, and believe it is their own actions that create such things in their lives, no one has a right to happiness or good luck,

I've never expected good luck, I don't believe in asking for it, but I also never asked for the bad luck, is it luck? Or is it fate? Is everything that happens to us destined? I don't have the answer to this but I am a great fatalist, I do believe in fate, and if fate deals me this hand then I have to go with it. I have to improve my odds myself, and one way to do that is not to feel sorry for myself, there are still so many people out there who are worse off than us.

I am startled out of my thoughts as Gary arrives back, he looks exhausted, he tries to smile at me, it's a very watered-down version of his smile, I tell him I missed him.

The Doctor is here, he tells me to sit, I sit on the edge of the bed and hold Gary's hand reassuringly. I can see the nurse watching me, she makes me feel very nervous, I am hoping there is no more bad news, I really don't need to deal with further bad news, the feeling of anticipation is making me shake inside, the thought of Gary having to deal with further negative news would stress me out.

The news is good, they feel he is stable enough to make the trip, oh the instant feeling of joy overtakes me, I move in closer I look into Gary's eyes, I give him my best smile and say, we are going back. He tries to smile, but with the paralysis to his face, it is very difficult for him, it's almost like he has forgotten how to do it, but he thinks he is smiling, that's all that matters.

The Doctor will talk to the Insurance Company, now I must wait for them to call and give me a plan, I have no idea of a time scale, but I hope it will be very soon. My desire to get out of here is so high I can't think of waiting for days, I don't know how to fill the days, how to occupy Gary's mind. There is no provision for therapy here, they just leave you in a room all day, he doesn't need food as he is drip fed, they attend mornings to prepare him for the day and again in the evening for bed, they change bottles and drips and that's about it.

Everyone leaves, we are alone, I talk to him about being ready to leave, I can't tell him the plan as I don't know it, I assume they will call in the morning, it's so hard, he can't ask me any questions, there just isn't a voice, I try to pre-empt any questions or fears he may have, I assure him they would not be taking him yet if it wasn't safe, they must do this all the time, they will have experts looking after us.

It's a very long and disturbed night, no sleep, the same terrors entering into both our worlds, mine probably different to his. I lay with him as always, holding him close, trying to comfort him, but knowing that I am ill prepared for this job. But I just chatter on, telling him we will get him better, trying to make sense out of something that has no sense. I tell him for the hundredth time, I am here, I will always be here, I ask him if he trusts me, he nods yes, I ask him if I have ever made a promise I didn't keep, he shakes his head, I ask him if I have ever lied to him, he shakes his head again, I say, then you have no reason to be afraid, my promises are watertight and I promise you we will win this fight and make it to our journey's end.

Nothing in life stays the same, everything has its moment, this time will be in the past one day, it will just be memories to look back on, we will remember the bad feelings less and less, we will choose what we remember about it ourselves, we will put the desperation we feel into a drawer in our memory close it and lock it, never to open it again, that's how self-preservation- works. we are not capable as human beings, of dragging too many harsh memories with us and still maintaining happiness in the future.

If you look back over your past, you will find that bad times in your life seem to fade a little, you know they happened but, often they do not seem as bad as they did at the time, if you don't allow this to happen, if you drag the same desperate feelings with you through your life, looking to blame someone or something, that's when you become bitter, and bitterness makes you ugly and unfulfilled, envious of other people's happiness, envious of other people lives, always feeling sorry for yourself. I will never be one of those victims of life's twists and turns.

DAY FIVE

The nights are dark by nature.
But the certainty is, the sky will
brighten and spirits will lift.
My spirits are high, and my wings are
Strong, to carry us higher, until his wings
strengthen and he can carry us both once again.

The sun peeks through the blind, morning has arrived, and the day will begin without us having to intervene. The nurses will be here soon and they will do their job and then I will exercise Gay until I get the much awaited call from the Insurance Company.

Gary is awake and ready for the day, the nurses have done their job and we are left alone again, I start to chatter on, for my own need as well as Gary's, I do our daily exercise with his leg, pushing, pulling, twisting, turning, anything to let him know it is still there, I raise his leg it is so heavy, I don't expect any response yet, I am fully aware it's early days, but what I do know for sure is that the earlier movement is achieved the better chance he will have, so I will continue until we get some experts on the job.

The call comes, it's 09.00 I was just about to go for a coffee. I am feeling quite relaxed, but not for long, is he really telling me that we are going today, later today, I ask stupidly, do you mean today? he does mean today.

I am told we need to be ready at 16.00 today. I thought we would have a lot more warning than this, I start to stress immediately, I have to get the car back to the house and pick up the case to take with us, I have to get someone to give me a lift back to the hospital, it's 09.10, he says he will call again later with precise details.

Now I am in a blind panic, I need to calm down and think straight, first I need to get my lift sorted, who can I ask, Alan, again, our biker friend I know he will help without question, I call him, he is only too happy to be able to help, I knew he would be, we are in the biker fraternity, they always help each other, a time is sorted to meet and the plan is set. I feel a little calmer already.

I have to wait until I have seen the Doctor, they need to do last minute checks and organise Gary's medication, I wonder how cold it will be at the other side, but they will make sure he is warm, I need to leave all that to the experts, I need to concentrate on my side of things fully. I start to work out the timings, a fifty- minute drive to the house and fifty minutes back, time to sort the house out, shut everything down and secure things.

The Insurance guy calls, they are moving the pick- up time to 14.00 hours as the weather is very windy and a storm is forecast later, my worst nightmare at this point, I start to panic yet again. He says the ambulance will pick us up, a doctor and nurse will meet us at the airport and accompany us on the flight, he tells me not to worry about anything, just be ready.

I need to leave now, I have to leave Gary and trust the staff to get him ready, how do I control my stress levels, I need to concentrate to drive, not panic too much, come on, I tell myself, take control, this is the easy part.

It seems so quiet at the house, the cases are still packed from Benidorm, I open mine and remove the summer clothes, replace them with a few warm bits I have there, the toiletries are packed so nothing to sort there, one case is ok as Gary has everything in Switzerland and I can't think past this.

Shutters down, power off, alarm on and house locked up, Alan arrives, one of his big smiles greets me and a friendly hug, I am very close to tears, too much kindness, he asks how I am doing and I say I'm ok, just anxious to get back to the hospital. I take a look back at the house, our lovely Spanish home and I wonder when we will see it again and hope that it will be safe.

We chat, it seems such a short journey, he has a calming nature, which suits me perfectly at this moment, another good friend to thank later. He drops me outside the entrance and his friendly face has so suddenly gone. I wonder when I will ever see him again, our life here in Spain has come to an abrupt end, and I have no idea if or when it will continue again, I can only hope that at some stage our life will resume with the friends we have made here, until then I will only look forward in this journey, no looking back for now.

When I get back to the room, Gary is barely awake, he has been heavily sedated, I wonder if I should be sedated, and smile to myself, knowing that I am serious about this, but I'm sure no one is actually taking me into consideration, I am just expected to deal with all this, maybe they do not even consider that this is also happening to me, and I haven't had any preparation for what is happening.

I have little knowledge of exactly what has happened in Gary's brain, of course I know what a stroke is, and I have faced someone having a stroke, but not this severe. One year prior to Gary's' stroke, my friend Maricela, had a stroke whilst we were out having lunch, it was pretty much like Gary's at the time, I stayed with her in the emergency room of this very same hospital, she had the same paralysis and speech loss, however, after 5 hours of the Doctor and nurses working on her arm and leg, she regained her mobility and speech, although somewhat confused and very poorly, she was allowed to come home with me the same day. I have thought about this so often, and know that Gary has not been so lucky,

his stroke was much more severe, but I still have hope that recovery can be achieved.

I take another call from the Insurance guy, he‘s just checking to make sure we are all ready, and that everything is on point with the hospital, as far as I know the answer is yes, he tells me again not to worry and I thank him for all his help.

Am I worried? Yes, I am, the weather as predicted has become grey and windy, and I am wondering how Gary will take the journey, I tell myself that they would not risk this if they were not one hundred percent sure it would all go ok.

The time arrives and the ambulance crew are here, it is a bustle of activity now, papers are signed, release forms and medication handed over, no goodbyes, no regrets at leaving, just a feeling of moving camp.

Gary is awake but very still, he understands what is happening, and just keeps his eyes on me, I do my best to look calm and reassuring, tell him that we are on our way to a new camp and the start of his journey to recovery, that we are together in this and we will succeed with our different strengths and our commitment.

We are moving on already and there will be no stopping us now, the journey is just beginning, we will be in Switzerland by the end of today, first he will go to the hospital in St Gallen, and more tests and assessments will take place, he has to be more stable before we can move to rehab. Before I can gather any more thoughts, we are at the airport.

It's so painful seeing my lovely husband so helpless on a stretcher, is he really fit for this journey? Such fear in his eyes, I have to go through a separate security check with our luggage, he is constantly searching for me.

I feel nervous, detached from everything I'm used to, I am usually so in charge and in control, now I am being directed by someone else, but in this instance It's a good thing, I'm not sure I would be able to think for myself enough to deal with all this officialdom.

The plane is waiting, it looks so small, it's very windy, actually cold. The doctor and the nurse meet us at the plane and introduce themselves, they are very friendly and welcoming, they are Swiss.

Gary has to be loaded on first, it's a difficult manoeuvre as the plane is so small, once he is on I follow, I immediately feel a little claustrophobic, Gary is, taking up the whole of one side of the plane, I sit in a middle seat on the other side next to him, the doctor behind and the nurse facing me. My knees are touching the nurses, it's so small, I can see the pilot and co- pilot, such a tight space. They secure Gary and I buckle up, neither am I good in confined spaces, or heights, but as they say needs must, this was never going to happen any other way, and if I am frightened, I can only imagine what Gary is going through.

I hold his hand as we take off, surprisingly smooth. Once in the air the nurse asks if I would like a drink, I feel like saying I would love a gin and tonic but of course I refrain from this and say no. I look around and wonder where she was even going to get a drink from.

She engages me in conversation, general conversation, where do we live, how long have we been in Switzerland, that type of thing, of course they have done this so many times they know how to put people at ease.

We have two hours twenty minutes to go, and the weather is getting very windy now, its magnified in such a small plane, I'm not usually nervous about flying but this is a whole new experience. The Doctor is very reassuring, it's a bumpy ride but that's our future journey for a while now, highs and lows, peaks and troughs, the highest mountain to climb together, never letting go of each other, sharing our strength, positivity and love, this journey will only end when we reach the summit and see the view from the top.

Gary seems fine considering. I think I am more nervous, but then again he is dosed up with drugs, the wind buffets us about quite a bit, I'm starting to feel a bit nauseous, wishing I had asked for a glass of water, this could be a long journey.

The Medical staff are so friendly, chatting and smiling, as if we are on a holiday jaunt to somewhere nice, the pilot joining in with info about where we are and how long we have left on this strange journey. I like this, I start to relax, I realise that this is the first time since this episode of our life started, that I have had a normal conversation with anyone, a conversation that wasn't about Gary or Gary's stroke, it's also what Gary has endured, every focus on him, no normal talk, like a blast of icy wind in my face.

I suddenly see things clearer, normality, that's the missing link to life at the moment, our normality has been swept away, he has to see some part of our life, our wonderful life, I have to see it also, I will never let this stroke define our lives, we will plan our future as we always have, I will never allow this to be stronger than me, and my strength will enthuse Gary along the way, I know this journey will be tough but we will become adventurers, facing storms but seeing rainbows at the end.

I am woken from my thoughts as the aircraft starts to make its descent into St Gallen airport, Gary is asleep, we are here in Switzerland, this is our home now, and I know we are not alone.

As I leave the aircraft an icy blast of wind blows through me, I don't have a warm coat on, just a jacket, as I stand on the tarmac waiting for them to disembark Gary, I start to shake uncontrollably, can't make my mind up if it's nerves or just the cold.

I can see people looking out of the departure lounge window, watching what is going on, they will be wondering what is wrong, who has been flown in by Air Ambulance, I think how curious we all are when we see tragedy happening around us. We never think it is going to be us, but one day suddenly it is. Believe me, you can never be prepared for it, but you can overcome the fear.

DAY SIX

Sometimes you must be lost in order to be found.
You have to fall, to learn how to get up.
You have to fail to eventually know success.
To keep climbing to reach your goal,
I found a little bit of sunshine, tucked away in Winter.
Grace and humility, I think they are called.
Location: Kantonsspital St Gallen Switzerland.

The Stroke

My first impression of this Hospital is its cleanliness, immaculate in every area. I feel very relieved, as Gary's immune system is very low, it was a constant concern to me in Spain.

His room is really nice, and they have put a bed in there for me so I can continue to stay with him, I will not leave him at this point, it's too soon.

There is a bustle of activity, smiling nurses and auxiliaries come and go, making Gary comfortable, explaining things to me about Gary's treatment, telling me he will be assessed tomorrow.

I feel lifted by their professional but friendly care. They explain that all my meals will be served in the room and I will receive a menu to fill in each morning, I feel so happy, I will be able to eat now. I would not like to know how much weight I have lost, but I know it's a lot, it's time I got some goodness back into my body, I need great stamina for this adventure.

We have everything we need for now; we are alone at last and it's time for me to have another conversation with Gary about this trip we are taking. I have to make sure that he knows I am here, fully committed to travelling this route with him, never leaving his side.

We are both tired, well actually I am exhausted again, so we will just watch the tv, no English-speaking channels so I find football, he is happy about that, a small smile. One that is not provoked by me, I can leave him for a few minutes, it's time for me to call his parents again, they need to have a proper update, not just texts. I put on my steady voice and I steel myself to sound optimistic, I have no further information for them other than he is comfortable, I feel very confident about this location.

I know they are relieved to hear from me, but none the less I can detect the concern and worry in Ted's voice, I tell him to tell Sylvia to try not to worry too much and to try to get sleep, easier said than done I know.

We try to relax for the evening, a meal is brought to me and it looks very nice, but I have no peace, it's so hard to eat and enjoy a meal when Gary is being tube fed by a drip, I find myself apologising for eating in front of him, he holds his hand out so I go to him and hold it, he squeezes it and his eyes say it's ok.

During the night, 'The Demons' enter again, Gary is in agonising thought, past life torturing his mind, I am awake and sense his pain, I climb onto his bed next to him and hold him close, he's trying to pull away from me, I can see him shutting down hour by hour. He needs something to hold onto, I give him my hand, I need more strength to pull him along with me, I wrap my arms around him, circling him in my love and commitment. I stay silent and still next to him, trying to keep him safe from the demons, willing him to sleep, he holds on one minute then pulls away the next. My strength in this moment is all I have to give. I need to give him every ounce.

Tomorrow is another big day, he will have scans on his throat and chest, I am very anxious of course, but also relieved that they are imminent. I don't like the cough he has; he didn't have it before. I am worried this is a problem with his respiratory system or is it due to the paralysis in his throat. I think again about this, how will he deal with life if he has to have a feeding tube, if he can't eat solid food, if he can't swallow to have a drink, I shake my head vigorously and throw these thoughts out of my head, no time for negative thoughts, it's not like me to go to that place, negativity is a long narrow corridor that has no doors to escape through and you can't see the end, it just gets darker the further you try to see down it, why would anyone want to be in that corridor.

It will be a full day tomorrow, scans first and then a therapist will come and see us and do assessments, I know these people will not just let Gary lay in bed all day, they will help us to understand what our next step is in his recovery.

The doctor will speak to me and we will get the results of all the tests tomorrow, I am told, and I am impressed with the efficiency of everything so far, I am feeling quite calm now, what a difference to how I felt in Spain, but of course that was right at the beginning of the journey, when I was full of uncertainty and sadness, now I have a great team around us, I can feel it.

I am so grateful when the morning arrives, the nights hold such dread for us, it's like clinging onto a ledge with your fingertips, hoping you will make it through without falling further into the black hole. If I fall, I will have to find another ledge to hang on to and it would be harder to climb back up, I must not fall further down.

A nurse arrives with my breakfast, served just as it would be in a hotel, the table is set for me and the food looks lovely, I am at last feeling hungry, but I have that terrible feeling for Gary, unable to enjoy any food, and having to suffer that terrible feeding tube up his nose, it just looks so uncomfortable. I say to him, I feel awful, but I am so hungry, and we both smile.

Whilst I eat they check Gary's feeding tube, and his Catheter, they chat to him and when this is all done, they proceed to change and wash him and make him comfortable in the bed, I can tell this is difficult for him, of course he is not used to having so many strangers around him, but he also knows it is necessary. It suddenly reminds me when us girls go for a smear test, it's so embarrassing and evasive, yet we put a brave face on, chat about our holidays or the family and smile through it, much the same for Gary for now, be brave little soldier.

Once I have eaten, everything is cleared away and someone comes to clean the room, she is Spanish, so we chat a little with the Spanish I have been learning, she is happy I can speak a little to her, and it is nice, she cleans with military precision, it feels so clean, I am so happy for this, my fears of cross infection melt away, we will be safe now.

Time for us to resume our exercises, he needs focus and so do I, I've been checking up on exercises I can do with his leg and arm, so we begin, his leg is so heavy, I place his foot on my chest, and bend his knee, I lean gently against it and ask him to push me away, I feel movement and he pushes slightly, that is it for me, I know we can do this. You don't have to be an expert to work this stuff out, you don't need any medical knowledge either, you just need the desire and determination to want to do it, to want to help this person that needs you to guide him.

Next a therapist arrives, I didn't expect that so soon, but I feel very happy inside, she tells me she wants to talk to us, and if I have any questions, she will try to answer them, her English is very good. Immediately I ask her about the exercises we are doing and is this ok, I show her, and she says yes, the earlier we start to move things the better, and she will give us more exercises to do. Until they have his next scan results, they won't do anything, but after that she will make a work plan and will attend him every day. I don't think anyone who hasn't experienced this situation, can possibly understand how it feels, to suddenly have such support it is like a huge weight being lifted off my shoulders, I feel I can breathe normally now. I am full of real hope today.

They will collect him after lunch and take him for his scan, till then I will just keep chatting and keep him as occupied as I can. TV and Football is part of the answer.

Our room is very comfortable, even with two beds in it, a table and two chairs, and an armchair, cupboard and drawers, there is a large bathroom with walk in shower and a separate toilet. We have a large window, which by the way is directly overlooking the Helipad, and beyond in the distance the mountains, I had forgotten how beautiful they look, I comment to Gary about them and he looks sad, I know it makes him think about skiing, I tell him to stop worrying about things that may never happen, he knows this is one of my biggest philosophies, if you worry about things now and then they never happen, you have spoilt today unnecessarily.

No one has told him he won't ski again, and I will never tell him that, so why worry about it now. No one knows what his future holds, not the doctors or therapists, no one can predict it, they can give an opinion, but they don't know his character or strength of will, it may be at a low ebb for now, but you can bet your life I will get that back soon enough. We will not dwell on negativity for one moment.

It's time, they arrive to pick him up for yet another scan, and then another talk with the doctor. Leaving me to unpack my things and settle in for who knows how long. Now I need to do some research that is needed, on which rehab clinic I think would be best for him. I can only go by reviews really, so I check out the top five, the number one in Switzerland happens to be only a thirty minute drive from where we currently live, perfect, I will speak to the Insurance Company, I have no idea what the criteria is or whether they will pay for my choice or whether they will want to decide, but this is the one for us.

I call the Insurance, tell the guy what I am thinking, and he says it's a great choice, so far so good, the only problem is that it is very popular, and they would have to hope for a place. At this moment we don't know when Gary will be ready to go to rehab, but he will set the wheels in motion. Again, I am so grateful to Gary's Insurance Company, we used to moan about the cost of his Private Medical Insurance, a legal requirement when working in Switzerland, but my goodness, you certainly get what you pay for in this instance. Another great feature is that I have one telephone number and I have one agent who is in charge of our case, I get to speak to him every time, none of this explaining the situation to a different person each time I call, he is so polite and sounds genuinely interested in how we are getting on.

Gary is back already, he looks so tired again, once he is settled, I tell him to sleep, I will leave him and go for a walk, I need some fresh air and to stretch my legs. On my return there is a note, explaining that I have a meeting with the Doctor at 16.00 hrs and someone will come to take me to his office. Instantly I feel a little nervous, that funny feeling you get in your stomach, like butterflies fluttering around, my face feels very flushed, and my hands are shaking a bit, then just in time an auxiliary arrives to ask if I would like a coffee, perfect.

I sit now to bring my daily diary up to date, which by the way I started on the first day of this journey, whilst Gary was in intensive care. It somehow relaxes me and helps me to see how we are moving forward every day, it may only be very small steps, but I know each day brings something new to us, each step moves us forward, further away from a very dark place, a place we will never return to.

The time moves on until someone comes to take me to my meeting with the Doctor, yes I am very nervous, it is such early days yet, I have no idea how much they can tell me about Gary's prognosis, what in their experience they can predict for his recovery.

I am hoping that they will have some good news about his throat, the tube is upsetting him all the time, it is so uncomfortable especially at night, I have to call the nurse every time, he catches it when he dozes off, it makes him feel nauseous so much of the time, and I am so afraid the paralysis won't go away, I need some clarification if this is the case, although I do not want to think about that outcome, I can only imagine how hard that would be to live with, so I have hope in my heart that this will not be the case.

It is a female Doctor, a warm smile on her face, she looks pretty relaxed, not as though she is dreading passing on bad news, we shake hands, she introduces herself and invites me to sit. Firstly, she says how sorry she is that we are going through this but, assures me they will be doing their best for us. I believe her. She then looks at her papers, and I take a deep breath and try to concentrate on her face.

The Stroke

The scan shows a large area of injury to the left side of his brain, well I know this already so that is no surprise, she tells me it affects the right side of his body, again no surprises there, I accept things so far with just a nod. She shows me the scan and points to the injury just above his ear, it looks like a large dark shadow, it looks so big, that does surprise me, I kind of thought it would be like a tiny spot, but I was way out with that one.

She explains that the injury is on the speech channel, which is why he can't talk, the injury goes out from there, affecting his arm and leg. She also explains that he has Aphasia, ok, I haven't heard of that and I ask her what it is.

Aphasia affects the cognitive skills, memory, recognition of objects, reading, writing, and on it goes, a whole list of things I can't even hope to remember. I remember thinking, God I hope she gives me a list of this stuff. She says they will test him to see just what stage it is at, I think to myself, well maybe it's a mild form of it, after all, he seems to know what is going on around him and he knows who I am, he is mourning his past life, so I convince myself it can't be that bad. Usually I am very good at seeing the best rather than the worse scenario, it has stood me in good stead in the past so I'm sticking with this for now on this one.

Next she tells me that he is incontinent due to a massive infection in his urinary tract, this is apparently very common with this stroke, and he will have to have the Catheter for now, I ask if this will get better, she says at some stage they will be able to get this sorted, the infection needs to clear, but this can take up to 12 months, but they can give him medication later to control things when the catheter comes out, that's good news, something positive to take back to him.

The scan shows that he has no peripheral vision, again I already know this but I ask if this will rectify itself, she says only time will tell. I press her for more information about statistically what chance does he have but she will not be drawn, she said he will have monthly eye tests, and there is nothing more they can advise. I think, absurdly so, that he will never be able to drive with this, then remember that he can't use his arm or leg. I remember, Gary used to joke and say, "when I retire, I'm not driving, you can do all the driving" well as I sometimes say to people, be careful what you wish for, it may not ultimately be what you want.

Good news is coming, his paralysis has gone from his throat, they will remove his feeding tube tomorrow, and his chest is clear, nothing to worry about there, it could just be the feeding tube, now that is really positive news for me to take back to him, I am elated, this will be so good for his mood and his move forward again to a better place. He will be able to eat again.

Suddenly I am feeling a bit overwhelmed with all this. I think she sees it, so she asks me if I have any further questions, I know I do but I can't think straight at this moment, I tell her this and she says she understands perfectly, she assures me she is always available and I can request a meeting with her anytime, but that she will be seeing me later in the week after the Physio has assessed Gary, I am happy with this for now.

Time to go back and give Gary some good news, anything but positive news is for my eyes only for now, and that includes Gary's parents and everyone else. Negativity has no value for anyone at this time.

I arrive back at the room to even more good news, he has a place at the Clinic we wanted, that's fantastic I tell him, and he looks pleased about it, we are due to be moved there in seven days' time, provided everything is all good with Gary, again, I have that feeling of calm but anticipation inside, it's a good feeling.

I talk about the things I have researched about the clinic thank goodness for the internet, I would be lost without it now, research is my new pastime, knowledge is power over this stroke, and knowledge will enable me to help Gary in his recovery, he deserves the best recovery possible and I need to stand by his side and make sure he never falters. I try to pass my enthusiasm and hope onto him, this will be our new camp for the next part of our journey to reach the top of the mountain, we will have experts to help, guide and support us, with their help we can rise to the challenge, I need to get my best climbing boots on.

We resume our exercises, progressing bravely to getting him to sit up, it's not hard for me to help him, swing his legs out, can he stand I wonder, I ask if he would like to try to sit in the chair, he nods, so here goes, both legs down, and I support him taking one small step to the chair, he sits heavily but he's made it, I can see it feels good for him to be sitting up.

A nurse appears, all smiles, she says that they can give him a shower, the first since this happened, that sounds wonderful, however, I'm not sure how this will work with all his drips etc, but they are expert at this so I am not concerned. I tell them I will go for a coffee to the coffee shop and reassure Gary that they need to do their job and I would only be in the way.

It's a good chance to make some phone calls, I need to update Ted and Sylvia with the positive news. News has now travelled to everyone and my Facebook page has a lot of good wishes and messages that I would like to read, whatever people say about social media, it is an excellent tool in situations like this. I try to sound cheerful, but of course I know his parents will see through that, I understand that they must be so worried, I'm sure they won't be sleeping, they will be agonising over the same things everyone does, why Gary? How did this happen? This isn't fair etc etc, and many more recriminations, it's human nature to look for a reason and try to understand, but in reality, there is no reason it's one person and not another, it's no one's fault, certainly nothing Gary did, the sooner we stop looking for answers the sooner we will accept it and move forward.

It's too early for me to tell them this yet, it would be insensitive of me not to allow them to feel upset, to grieve for their sons' misfortune, they have every right to feel cross, every right to question why and certainly every right to think this is not fair, only I can move forward from this fast, if not these thoughts will just clog my mind up, and I am here with him, he needs me to be clear to think, clear to work with him, this is not a time to let him stay in a bed with too much time to think, and not a time for me to dwell, in self- pity, I have no time for such unpleasantry.

It's time to settle into our new home for the next week, we have lots of time to build confidence, time to relax a bit together, Gary is happy that he can shower every day and that his catheter will be removed during the day and he can use the toilet, providing he can give enough warning to get him there, and he will stay out of the bed after his shower. It is a time to find out how strong his leg is, how much movement we can promote with exercise, there will be no giving in to this. If anyone tells me he won't walk again, I will tell them, that will not happen on my watch.

I am surprised at how positive I feel, how strong I feel, I know this strength is there for Gary, and I will be able to encourage him, I need to enthuse some of my determination into him, at night I feel him drawing away, I know what he's thinking, he's feeling sorry that this has happened to me, he is hurting for me, because he is that type of character, he is worried that my life is going to take the toll, he's probably thinking, "she won't want this life with me", he thinks about the wonderful life we have, with so much in it, and he is thinking that is all gone now.

I have to address this quickly, he has to save his energy for recovery, not for feeling sorry, honesty is the best wake-up call I could give him right now. I won't allow him to feel sorry for me when I don't, that's just a non- starter.

He is my soul mate, he has been since the first day we met, we have always been committed to each other and nothing will or can change that.

DAY SEVEN

After what has now become the normal sleepless night, awful bed wetting, his bag is full or the catheter has fallen out, so upsetting for him, the staff are brilliant, someone is there in an instant when I ring for them. No fuss, just professional, but still it is intensely distressing for him, and the same for me to watch him. The bed has to be changed two or three times a night, and I selfishly think to myself, how would I cope with this at home, then I think, that's normal anyone would think this, and I'm not at home, and this is going to be temporary, so dismiss those thoughts very rapidly.

Both fed, showered and dressed ready for the day ahead, the sun is shining, the view is magnificent and Gary is sitting in "A" wheelchair, I won't say his wheelchair, because it isn't, it's on loan for now. There is never a moment that I waste contemplating that he will stay in a wheelchair, and I tell him this, I take his face in my hands and I look him straight in the eyes, I ask him, do you believe me,? He hesitates so I say, do you understand what I am saying? He nods his head, so I say it again, do you believe me? He still hesitates to respond, so I continue with, if you don't believe me then you don't really know me after all this time, is that true, he smiles mostly with his eyes, and nods his head, so if you know me, you trust me to keep my word then, he nods again, now we are getting somewhere. Today is the first day of me being the teacher and you being the good student I tell him, all you have to do is remember at all times that I am always right, now the smile has reached his lips, a bit crooked but none the less still cute. I feel he is coming back to me, and I can work on this.

He has a drip stand connected to him, but we can work around that, it's time to see how he can stand, I support him and he uses his good side to rise from the chair, lean on me I am stronger than I look my love, I tell him to take one step with his left leg, he does, very tentatively, I manoeuvre his right leg forward a few inches, he is trying not to lean on me too much, that's good, we repeat the same thing, he's upright and fairly steady, this could be at the fear of overbalancing me, but it will make him stronger, we make it for about two feet, then back. I ease him into his chair and he lets out a big breath, he is exhausted, but I tell him how great that was, and every day we will, build on it. I am personally over-joyed, just seven days after a severe stroke he is upright and kind of shuffling, I feel we need a pat on the back.

He wants to have a rest, so back on the bed for him, he has earnt it, small steps that's a great start. I can go to the coffee shop and have a drink and contemplate things. I have always been good at that, and also pride myself at being a good planner. Gary used to always say, you are never happy if you haven't got a plan brewing, and he was so right. So, armed with my diary and notepad, I am off to make plans. The coffee shop is so nice, the food looks fresh and lovely, it reminds me of the restaurant at Ikea here in Switzerland.

I decide we can't just concentrate all our energies on his leg, we have to also get his brain to communicate with his arm. A lot of people, of course, don't understand what a stroke does, why would they, if they haven't had to think about it, or been faced with it, what I know is that there is no injury to his arm or leg, I describe it like this: Gary's mother board is still intact, the part where his emotions, morals and understanding are, some of his wires are crossed and even disconnected, preventing the brain from moving his right side, his circuit board is damaged, mainly on the speech channel, preventing his words from getting through. We can and will untangle the wires, we can and will re-connect the brain with the muscles, we can and will see the damage to the speech channel repairing itself, although we don't know how long this will take or how much the injury will repair, but we can do therapy to help this. His mother board needs no work whatsoever, his heart is undamaged and just as big as it ever was, he loves us and cares about us just as he always has, we just ask that everyone who loves us, supports us on this journey any way they can.

Today I have seen a brief glimpse of the old Gary, this is a great start and he will be drawn back where he belongs, his smile is still there for me, I know he is trying so hard to hold his feelings inside, keep his thoughts hidden, but I know his every thought, I have them for him, but I am stronger to push them away. Every day there will be struggles to overcome, but we will overcome them with humility. I will be right by his side for every step, if he flounders, I will be there before he falls, I will never allow him to feel alone for one minute, I will be his sanity in this madness.

The evenings are filled with my lovely meal, poor Gary sits at the table with me, and patiently has to watch while I eat, but tomorrow we hope this will change when they remove his feeding tube. Then TV to occupy his mind, he loses himself in the football briefly, berating me with an expression on his face or a hand gesture when I ask those ridiculous questions, why do they wear long shorts under short shorts, that kind of thing, I like to do it to promote a reaction, and I'm happy when it does, it's all about getting as much normality into this as I can.

When the time comes for bed, I now get him ready, I know what to do and can replace his catheter, so I walk him to the toilet for his last pee of the day, I leave him alone in private, then he sits on a chair to do his teeth. As much independence, even at this early stage is paramount for his wellbeing, I am his wife, his lover and his best friend not his mother, and he must always feel that, I will not treat him like a small child, that would be disastrous, I have seen other people go down this route and it never ends well.

If I said I didn't dread the nights I would be lying, so I won't, there is little sleep to be had, the terrors return every night, even though I have asked for stronger sleeping pills they never help, so now, instead of trying to make him sleep, I get him out of bed and into a chair, make him comfortable with pillows and blanket and the same for me, I ask the night staff for a cup of tea, which she is happy to do, and she chats for a while with us, she gets to know who we are, which is nice.

I have started to show him all the lovely wishes and comments on my Facebook page, and talk about how supportive our friends are, and I scroll through the day's postings, it's a great way of distracting us. If he dozes in the chair, it's a bonus and he is comfortable, if I doze it's a miracle! I have decided that there is no point in trying to lay in bed counting the hours, far better to spend quality time together, even in this situation.

We make a plan for tomorrow and I ask him how he would feel about me taking him in the wheelchair downstairs to the coffee shop as the forecast is nice, we have to go outside to the next building, he nods yes, so I will ask the nurse tomorrow.

The morning arrives as inevitably as the night does, our routine commences and we are getting very good at doing everything ourselves, I leave him on the shower chair to shower himself, then I dry him, and after he's dry, he walks to the sink and sits to do his teeth, it's a struggle, he's not used to using his left arm, but we feel great achievement once it's done. I shave him and that's pretty disastrous, I can't get the pressure right, I am frightened of cutting him, but feel it is better than nothing. He looks a bit disgruntled and I tell him to get on with it and he can learn to do it left-handed soon enough.

The nurse does not hesitate, she thinks it is a nice idea to go to the restaurant, but all his drips have to be transferred to the wheelchair, so I ask her to show me what to do, as I will then do it myself. It's not hard, just need to remember where everything goes, but if I get it wrong, she tells me it will bleep in the nurse's station.

Off we go, we take the lift down and then outside, it feels like freedom, fresh air and sunshine, on our faces, its November and it's warm. I put Gary at a table and go to get a coffee, feeling sorry that he can't have anything, but I know he is happy for me. Today, after a final check he will be free of his feeding tube, I am so grateful for this, it's just so restricting and truly horrible for him to endure.

We pass a pleasant half an hour, chatting and people watching just like we always did, I make him laugh with my descriptions of everyone, no one takes any notice of us, there are sick people, lots with drips just like Gary everywhere, we are just part of the crowd.

Time to return and see when he will be ready for his next step forward in this episode of our lives. No news yet, so it's time for our walk practice, first I will try to transfer the drips, I feel confident I remember the routine, two minutes and it's successful, a gold star for me, I tell Gary and he puts his thumb up and smiles.

I tell him we will walk to the window and we can sit in the sunshine, and wait for the doctor, he looks nervous, but I tell him he can do it and I will not let him fall, he trusts me, of course he does, I have never let him down yet, it's a little struggle getting up from the chair but we do it, I support on one side and he slowly shuffles across the room to the window, see, I told you so, I say, what a team we are, and he gives me the thumbs up again.

I think about his speech at this point and wonder, if he can make any sort of noise, as I haven't heard anything at all yet, I wonder, has his voice actually gone or just the power to get the words out, I make a mental note to check up online later, there is so much I need to understand about this.

I tell him that I am writing a diary and that one day I will have it published, he wants to see it, but I tell him it's not the right time yet, I will know when the right time comes, it's too raw at the moment, he settles for that.

Time passes until the doctor and a nurse arrive, suddenly I feel very nervous, frightened if it isn't time and he is disappointed, frightened of the procedure to remove it, I'm sure it can't be pleasant, but also certain it will be quick.

I start to imagine what it will be like to have it removed, then I quickly dismiss those thoughts, I don't need to go there. Everything is going on calmly around us, I hold his hand and tell him to focus on me, he stares at me, I try to distract him with idle conversation.

The doctor tells us what is going to happen, he says it will make him gag but it will be fast. It is done just as he predicted, I am so happy for him, he was so brave, and the doctor congratulates him, well done Gaz I say. They explain that he will have to start gradually on liquids first then yoghurt, until he can swallow properly, and his throat heals from the tube, that's fine, we are very patient as long as these things are improving.

They offer him a drink to check if he can swallow, just a sip, a little difficult but the doctor says it's normal for now. The doctor asks how I am, and I tell him I am great, and I thank him. Gary needs to rest now, and it's time for me to make a few phone calls again. I leave him to sleep and I go to the coffee shop again where I find a quiet corner.

It's time for a long chat with my dear friend Jackie, although she has her own cross to bear with her husband who has Alzheimer's, she has been a constant support for me, and a reminder also that other people have difficult lives, she is one of the strongest women I have met, and I have the ultimate respect for her.

I know she will be one of the people who understands more than most, how life changing this is for us. She is unaware of how strong she is, she never accepts praise easily, and those are the things I love about her, she never makes it about herself, she is never a victim, she just gets on with it. I know Jackie will be a source of comfort and encouragement along our journey.

It is a very easy call, we chat about Gary's progress and she is happy to hear, but we also do the usual gossip about what is happening in the village, she tells me that everyone is so shocked to hear our news and passes on their best wishes, I ask her to thank them. Momentarily, I feel a stab of pain in my heart, our home in Spain seems so far away, in distance and time. I wonder again, if and when we will ever be able to return to that life.

I return to Gary still sleeping, he does not look relaxed or comfortable, how could he, one side of his body with no feeling. I sit beside the bed, and bring my diary up to date, then I sit and watch him, he looks the same, he's just my husband, but he is injured and hurting physically and emotionally, he doesn't feel the same I know that, but I also know we have only just started our journey and we have all the time it will need to reach our summit. We have the most important thing we need, that is commitment to each other, and respect for each other's life. We are as important to each other as we are to ourselves. Being in love means putting the other person first.

DAY EIGHT

It is his own hurt that will create the strength
of his power to heal.
Once we are broken, we will never be perfect again,
But we were never perfect before.
As long as we mend enough to be happy,
perfection is no loss.

Anyone who looks for perfection in someone else will always be disappointed, if you look for perfection in yourself then you will never be happy with yourself.

The most perfect people are the ones who don't expect perfection, the ones who don't have to strive for perfection in themselves or others, just accepting where you are at that moment in time, will give you the most satisfaction.

I will always be a part of this adventure with Gary. His imperfections were always the quirky things about him I love, and a stroke will not take those away, a stroke does not take the person away unless you allow it to. If you allow the stroke to drive you away, then it is your own weakness not the stroke, it's all about staying strong and having the commitment to hold that persons hand when things are really tough, finding the strength yourself to allow them to lean on you, until they find their own strength again.

Gary is dealing with his daily routine now, we are comfortable with our surroundings, we are familiar with the staff and temporary friendships are forged, we are lucky we are in such a safe environment, if we need anything we only have to ask.

Gary will have one of his medication drips removed today, eventually he will have tablet medication, this will be added to our daily routine, some probably forever, certainly blood thinning medication, neither of us is used to this, but we will get used to it.

Today, we will venture out of the room for our walk, a shuffle around the corridors, as I call it, he is very weak and unsteady but determined, as much for me as himself, I do know that, he wants to make me happy, and he does.

It's often good to allow someone to fight for you and not just themselves, it's important to take the focus away from the problem and give them a solution to it for a period of time. You know that thing when you say, don't do it for me do it for yourself, well this is the opposite, don't do it for yourself, do it for me, it's called reverse psychology, and it works for us.

We make it round the corridor quadrangle, as we pass by the nurses station, they look very surprised to see us, they all wave and smile, Gary gives the thumbs up, he is smiling, a real broad Gary smile, we are treading our path, making our route, there is no turning back now, we completed our first trip. We are truly on our way, and there will be no stopping us now.

Back in the room, and ready for a rest, I smile and say, one small step for mankind, one massive step for you. I make sure he is comfortable, it's the time he gets a little sleep, when the light is there, when the darkness can't get to him, when the terrors can't creep under the door, when he has a little peace from all this tragedy, healing comes with sleep.

It's Friday, the doctor will come to check up on us before he leaves for the weekend, for now I have my phone calls to make, and my cup of coffee in the coffee shop, it's good to just get out of the room, and spend a little time chatting on the phone.

Back in the room, I quietly sit and write an entry into my diary. When this all happened, I only had a work diary of Gary's to use, it strikes me for the first time, how funny it is, not a conventional diary, it has pictures of grain, rice and seeds, pictures of cakes and chocolate, machinery and buildings, I think how nice it would be to publish it in its original form, but quickly the idea seems ludicrous.

I find myself watching Gary sleeping, hoping he is at peace for a while, I can't remember when I slept properly or comfortably, I am just on autopilot, but by nature I don't need much sleep and now that seems such a blessing for the months ahead, the strong sleeping tablets don't seem to work, the night terrors are so strong, they can't be fought, not for now, he will take his sleep when he can, and I will watch over him through the night.

The Stroke

I try so hard to take the fear away during his nights, but I fail, I feel desperate and hopeless to help, I can't make it right when the dark engulfs us, when the silence of the corridors outside leave us to our thoughts, no distractions, no relief from the demons in our heads. My head is full of demons, my own demons. I try not to let them enter but it's hopeless, they creep into my mind, they permeate my thoughts the very second I close my eyes, if I am suffering from my own thoughts then what is he suffering, unspeakable torment, a voice he can't use, a body that is failing him, a future that he cannot see, a past that he cannot let go of.

I see the light of dawn moving outside the window, morning is coming to rescue us, we cling to each other till the morning comes, then he falls asleep.

I leave him to sleep, it's time for me to get ready, I feel weary, but I know that will pass, it's not time for me to rest yet, my time will come.

It's the weekend, no doctors, no tests, we have the time for ourselves and I will fill it with laughter whenever, however I can, it may only be fleeting moments but, those moments will be precious, for now, I will encourage his walking, there is no stopping now we have started, and we will go to the coffee shop where he is allowed to have a juice, it's the weekend that's what we do.

For the first time since November 2nd he will get dressed, whatever normality I can bring to his life, I will find it.

He is so happy to get into his clothes, even though it is only a tracksuit, difficult operation, disconnecting tubes, running them up sleeves, making sure everything is free from obstructions, but we manage, now we have a portable stand to take with us, it's not technical, we've all seen them on the TV, children wheeling them around with smiling faces, and it's a great prop to lean on.

I tell him we will walk to the coffee shop, he looks very dubiously at me, he points to his catheter laying idle on the floor, he's worried about needing the toilet, but I have already located every toilet on route, he smiles, knowingly, because really he knew I would do that, so he resigns himself to his walk.

I tell the nurse what we are planning, asking her in a manner really, she say's if she can't trust him with me then she can't trust him with anyone, I take it as a yes and tell her she is correct. He holds my hand, I squeeze it tight, I tell him he is safe, he gives me a look that says, I know, and off we go, slow but sure, with measured steps, the fresh air is warming with the sun, we sit for a moment just outside on a bench, It's a long trip for him, with only me for a safety net, in reality it is a two minute walk.

One of his nurses see us and stops to remark how great it is to see him dressed, and outside in the fresh air, I say, we are on a date, it's the weekend and we are going for a drink, Gary puts his thumb up and she smiles.

The coffee shop is busy with weekend visitors and patients all trying to escape the confines of their hospital rooms, I remark that someone has taken our table, how dare they, this makes him giggle, just to hear the sound, is like a prize I have won, it's that moment I mentioned earlier, it's fleeting but memorable.

He drinks his orange juice through a straw, I can tell it's like nectar to him, it dawns on me, that there will be a lot of things that he took for granted, everyday things that are now just simply impossible for him to contemplate, we need to find the knowledge for him to process these everyday things again. Everything, every detail of his life is still there, trapped for now, but we will open it up again., I will never stop questioning and learning, he is my life's work now.

We make our way back ready for lunch, he is excited about his food, it's good to see him want to eat, he looks so thin , he has lost so much weight, he needs building up, he will need all the strength he can find. We have soup to start, it tastes delicious, but I'm sure that is part due to eating without guilt, and enjoying watching him eat, although it is nice. His main course is pureed but they shape everything separately, so it is not just like porridge, his meat is shaped like a steak, it makes us smile, they have done everything to make it good for him. he doesn't eat too much, but he enjoys what he does, on the other hand I eat everything with relish and enjoy every mouth full. We finish with ice cream and a cup of tea.

We both rest after lunch, he sleeps, I just rest, sleep will not grace me, my thoughts ever lively, thinking, thinking, it's like having something racing around inside my head, trying to escape, but never finding a way out.

He wakes, silently at first, I don't hear him, then he touches my hand, and he smiles, he hates the catheter, he wants to go to the toilet, no time to call for the nurse so I remove it and help him to the bathroom, it's amazing the things you can do, that previously you would have said no way to, now I just get on with it.

We change over to the portable stand again, and we are off for a shuffle around the corridor, a young student nurse joins us, and comments how well he is doing, I agree with her, and I am proud.

This has been a very positive day, walking slow but sure, whatever the future holds, for now this is something that we will build on.

Over the days there has been a slight movement in Gary's right arm, although I notice it is instigated from the shoulder lifting, there is no actual movement in the arm itself. I told the nurse and she is contacting the physio, but she says this is normal, it's time for yet another assessment.

I need to learn much more about this stroke to be able to help Gary, I won't be a bystander in his recovery, and I have the World on the internet at my disposal, I need to understand exactly how Gary's brain is working and more about the injury, of course I will be able to ask all my questions when we get to the Rehab Clinic later, they are the true experts and they will be able to answer all of my questions I am sure of that. Till then, I will research as much as I can.

For now, each day will be full of positivity and exercise, he is so happy when he walks, it's very slow of course and I have to support him, I am afraid of him falling, his balance is not good and the leg is not strong, but it is amazing that he is walking already, everyone here seems very surprised to see us walking the corridors and going to the coffee shop. I long for the day when he has no drips to accompany him, and we won't be going to Rehab until that is done, I am here to make his nights less fearful and his days pro- active and positive. So, for now this is our home and we are as happy as we can be in this situation.

DAY NINE

Take my hand, it is steady I can guide you.
Hear my heartbeat, it is strong, its beats for two.
Look into my eyes, they are clear, they see the way.
Look at my smile, it's joyous, it will cheer your mood.
Look no further each day, than you and me, there will be no tears.
We are still us, together, as it has always been.

Our experts are getting us ready for the next part of our journey, the time is not quite right yet, Gary is not prepared or strong enough to move camps. We both need a little more preparation and we will obtain that here, in this safe place, with the help of these wonderful people, and through each other. This camp is on level ground, no fear of sliding down the slope, falling or losing our way, and lots of friendly people with good advice and promising words. I am not looking up to the summit ahead, as I know it will look high and difficult, the time will come for me to face this challenge but for now I am taking this time to gather my thoughts and put everything in place.

Gary has more swallow tests today and they are happy with them, so we are looking forward to the day he can eat a proper meal, but he needs to take his time as there is a threat of choking, so he will have to take things very slowly, so no chances to take there.

The therapist teaches us hand and arm movements to practice, they seem totally disconnected from his brain, there is no movement or feeling at all, this is very disturbing for me, but it is such early days and we will start with them immediately, she says we are doing great things with his leg and walking and to carry on. I tell her I want to try him on the stairs, and that I have already checked that he can get up a step, she says she will come with us now and help.

The stairs are a difficult manoeuvre, it's not just needing the power to push on the leg, it's convincing the brain to do what you want it to, we spend half an hour, then he is tired, so back for a rest. I have time to think about what muscles he needs for stair climbing, and how we can get the brain to recognise them.

The Stroke

Gary does not sleep for long, he wakes and has tears in his eyes, it is so heart-breaking to see someone you love, once so strong and confident, and in control of his life, unable now to control the tears. Tears of frustration and fear, and things I can only try to understand. I have tried to put myself in his place, but the thoughts were so dark that I had to stop that. I am afraid to give him a hug in case I cry also, my emotions are very near to the surface of course, so I talk, telling him that I understand what is going on in his head, and it is better to get up now, he is just looking at me, I have to coax him off the bed.

Once he is in his chair, I suggest the restaurant for a drink, he shakes his head, Ok I say, then let's just go for a walk round the corridor, again a negative shake of his head. Now he isn't looking at me, no eye contact, he's shutting down again, I see the signs and I know this is dangerous for him.

I have a thought, I ask him if he would like me to call his parents and they can talk to him and he can listen, his reaction is instant, he leaves me in no doubt that this is not going to happen, I calm him and tell him it was just a thought, and I will call them later, myself. That was not one of my better ideas. He does not want to do any exercises, I try to coax him to come and sit at the table and we can get a drink here, but no, he closes his eyes and shuts right down, as if he has blocked me completely. I have to leave him and go outside to think and stop my heart from beating so fast. This is not good. I feel cross with him, let down, does he think I don't have dark thoughts, does he think it is easy for me. Instantly I feel guilty, of course, I know that those thoughts are part of why he is feeling so desperate.

I sit on a bench outside, there is no sun today, and it's cold, I like it, it's sharp and my body reacts to it, it makes me aware of my senses, I start to shiver and I just sit there, maybe 10 minutes, then I am really cold, I have to force myself to stand up and go back inside, the doors open and as I walk in, the warm air hits me, instantly I want to turn around and go back outside, I want to walk, I want to be alone, I have images going on in my head, I see myself running, faster and faster, someone is calling me but I won't turn to look, it's like I am frightened to see who is calling, I run faster, but the voice gets louder and louder, no matter how fast I run I can't escape the voice, I can't see anything in front of me it's just a white mist all around me. Suddenly I recognise the voice, it's mine, I need to stop running and go back.

I walk into his room, I am smiling, I feel calm. I go to him and put my arms around him and tell him everything is going to be ok, I tell him I share his pain and I will share that pain every day until the pain goes away, I tell him I do understand how he feels, because this didn't just happen to him, it happened to the both of us and we will survive. Not just survive but rise up mended and strong again, he will be complete again, but he needs to fight for me, he needs to help me on this journey too, we are in it together, and only walking side by side can we reach the view at the top of the mountain. I realise I needed to go out into the cold to come back into the safety of the warmth. We are one again, he will be ok again for now.

He points at his shoes, and we are back on our track, he tries to smile at me but the tears flow, he reaches for my hand and holds on tightly, I know he wants to speak but can't, I look at him and say, don't let this bloody stroke beat us, we are stronger than it, and I am stronger than you for now so lean on me and feel safe.

I tell him I know he has dark thoughts, about will he, won't he get his life back, on track, but no one knows, how much of his life will come back. But I believe our thoughts have to ultimately be controlled by ourselves, the effects of the stroke, we have to work hard at, we must never give in to doubts, doubts will sap your strength just as surely as recrimination, they are all useless emotions and they will win if you let them. Again I tell him, the door to our past life is closed, it can never be opened but we can find a new door to a new life, a life that we will make just as good, but for now we have to concentrate on the present, we need to live in the present, the here and now, one moment at a time, forget everything that has been, we are heading somewhere we have never been, and we will make it our time no matter how hard.

The day got so much better, I made him wet shave with his left hand, and it was much better than when I did it, he was so happy, he's smiling again, little positive steps, make big differences.

When the nurse comes to check on us, he touches his face, so I tell her what he has done, she says it looks great, and she is very impressed with him, he looks full of vanity and pride, and melts my heart. This makes him a little more independent, another move, forward.

We receive great news, out of the blue, we are to be moved to Rehab tomorrow, his remaining drips will be removed in the morning and we will move to our next campsite, I have every emotion all in one moment, trepidation, excitement, fear, worry. I ask him if he understands what is happening, he doesn't look sure, I often wonder if he understands what is going on around him, sometimes he shows no reaction to things, and this is one of those times, and that's strange for such momentous news, so I explain it to him slowly, now I can see that he understands, I tell him this is the best news, very exciting, proper therapy with experienced people who are trained to help him, I don't give him time to lapse into melancholy I keep talking, this is the next chapter, we are truly going to step foot on the mountain and start climbing to the top. It's time for us to get our climbing boots on and gather all our equipment ready to grab this adventure and make it ours.

Our usual dark night engulfs us, maybe a little worse if that is possible. I try so hard as always, to take the fear away, I fail, I have feelings of sheer desperation. He has the strongest sleeping medication he is allowed at this point, so that is not the answer, his nightmares are too strong to control.

We sit for a while and I read to him, he gets restless so we go for a walk around the silent corridors, the night staff, kind as always make us a drink, Gary can have a warm drink now, but the paralysis makes it difficult for him to control his mouth, so he has a straw, he still enjoys it. Again, peace descends upon the day, almost as though the daylight makes everything safer, and the bustle of people around means we are not alone. After his shower he lays on the bed to sleep a little, our routine is easy, and the days have been passing moderately fast.

Sometimes he picks something up, he studies it almost like he is trying to remember what it is, he has no concept of the difference between a knife and a fork, he tries to eat his soup with a fork, he can't use the TV remote, I'm not certain that he can read, but I don't pursue this for now, I don't want to draw attention to anything we are not sure about.

He is better able to communicate his needs to me without speaking now, we are a team, a unit, we understand a look, an expression, a gesture, I need to keep his mind away from his speech loss for now. I have the ability to decompartmentalise aspects of his disabilities, put them in a separate box and close the lid for now, I don't have any information to assist me with what the possibilities are, so I won't think about them just now. It's better to focus on the things that we can improve.

As I sit in the room, by the window and write my diary, I look up to see him watching me, he is smiling and I see a glimpse of Gary, I go to him and he wants to give me a kiss, it is a gentle kiss, full of meaning, it's a thank you just for being there, I tell him I am here and will never be far away, he squeezes my hand and my heart almost misses a beat, he is still the same person inside, still my caring and loving husband, no change there, I am grateful he is still here with me.

By now a lot of people are used to seeing us walking around, everyone is cheerful and stops to chat to us, calling us both by name, even when they don't speak English, it's the universal language of hand gestures and eye contact. It occurs to me that it could be very difficult if the therapists at the Rehab clinic don't speak very good English, then I brush the thought away, but make a mental note to ask about this.

Our day is filled with short walks, and drinks in the coffee shop, it just seems like a little bit of normality, in this madness.

Gary gets very upset about his incontinence, and I can only imagine how that feels for him, I reassure him that once the infection clears up that will sort itself out, I have no idea if this is a fact but I am not going to tell him otherwise, truth sometimes has no place over human feelings. The desire to make someone feel better is far stronger than the small deceit, and anyway, it could be perfectly true, I haven't been told otherwise, so I am at peace with it for now.

There is a note waiting for us, we have a meeting with the Director, she is going to give us an update, this is always welcome to me, I am always looking forward to our move to Rehab and dreading it at the same time.

She arrives, prompt as always, and I smile inwardly, thinking to myself, well they do make the best time pieces in the World, so they have no excuse to be late, I think how young she looks, but then remember, that you know you are getting older when the policemen look young, I think this is a similar analogy.

So the news is very promising, they will test his levels, such as Magnesium, Potassium, Vitamin D, and the list goes on, all things that are crucially affected by a stroke, he will have a swallow test, and if that is positive he will go onto solid food. She says they need to get him into the best condition they can before they will move him, I find this very reassuring. She asks me if I have any questions, I say I have a hundred, but I can't think of one right now, it makes her laugh, and she says, yes I understand, if you think of one you can call me. She says she has seen us walking outside and we are doing an amazing job. If she is happy with all the tests, then our move will go ahead. I am elated, anxious and worried, each emotion vying for top spot, wondering why I have no questions at such a momentous time.

His tests will start at 09.00 tomorrow, and the Doctor will bring them and discuss them during the afternoon, a big day tomorrow We could be leaving this camp to go to our new one very soon. I am nervous, no, I am terrified, to some extent, Gary will be living there, it will be his home for some time, I will have to leave him every night, I can't think about this just yet.

When she has left, we settle down to a cup of tea and make a start on a box of Swiss chocolates that have arrived from Gary's Company, along with a card, signed by his colleagues. He manages to suck a couple of soft chocolates to death and thoroughly enjoys them, I read the messages out, he cries a little and so do I, lovely heart-warming messages. Most people, I don't know, of course, I was not really involved with Gary's workplace, only meeting people once a year at the Xmas get together, and never really feeling getting to know anyone. We have had many messages and cards, names I have never heard, I show them to Gary, he looks puzzled at a lot of them, which I think is strange, but don't overthink it. There is such an element of shock in the messages, but of course there would be, this was so sudden and so unexpected, you could not have predicted this two weeks ago.

I think back to today, about our trip down on the elevator, I asked Gary to press the button for floor eight, he studied the key pad, but just shook his head, I pointed to it, he looked nervous, so I pushed it, I let it go, but now I am wondering about it, so I ask him if he wants to read some of the text messages he has had on his phone, I open one and pass it to him, he just looks and shakes his head, it's confirmed, he cannot read, I casually take it back and read a few, but inside I am churning this over, something else his brain injury has affected, and I have no idea if this will improve.

Research, research, my best friend the internet, at least I can get some sort of perspective on it, accepting that every case is different.

I think that Gay is mostly unaware of the brain injury side of things, he doesn't even seem to realise that he has no peripheral vision, he just turns his head to compensate, he seems more aware of his physical disabilities, I suppose this is typical, as he can see and feel his limbs but his internal injuries are such that he seems oblivious to them, maybe this is a complete saving grace for both of us for now.

We will have a lot more to face once we leave here, the real journey will begin, this is just the preparation, getting him fit and strong enough to be able to cope with the trek ahead. It's not going to be a walk in the park, it's going to be like boot camp, he will need focus, and belief in himself and his ability to overcome what may seem like insurmountable obstacles. I too need to be able to let him find his strengths and overcome his weaknesses, but most of all he needs to know that I am here for the whole journey.

ME

Pauline Yates

Maybe it's time I gave a brief profile of myself. I am nothing out of the ordinary, I came from a working-class background, my father was English my mother Irish, she came over to Britain when she was 17. Neither one of them was highly educated but they were hard working. My father was extremely, naturally talented musically, he could play any instrument without ever having had a lesson, he wrote poetry, and was very artistic, I am creative and I attribute this to him.

I can't say I had a happy childhood, or homelife and I attribute this to my mother. We never got on as mother and daughter and that remained the situation throughout her life, she did not like my happy relationship with my father and that caused a lot of upset and pain.

I had a basic education to the age of 15, I was keen to learn and was in the Alpha stream throughout my secondary school, but I was never expected to go on to further education, so, I left school at 15, with no exams under my belt.

I had belief in myself when no one else did, I had ambition when I didn't even know what that meant, and I had a burning desire to do better in life. I was not beautiful by any measure, but I was pretty and personable, and I had a style of my own, that made me stand out in a crowd, I would carry this with me to the present day. I had an air of confidence that I didn't always feel, but I had a strength within to stand up for myself and not let my insecurities show.

My first job was in a hosiery factory, if you kept your head down and worked hard the money was good, there are aspects of my life at that time that I do not want to visit in this book, this book is about Gary's journey. But I think it is important to understand who I am.

I did work hard for three months and I said, earnt good money, most of which I saved for my future plan, which was to be a hairdresser. I took a Saturday job in a salon, and I knew that one day I would train, which eventually I did, and I promised myself I would have my own salon, which I did.

Life wasn't always easy, but I was a fighter and I never gave up once I had my mind made up. If I, or anyone else, ever set me a challenge, no matter how big or small, I saw it through to the end, I am strongminded, and if anyone ever tells me it won't work or I won't succeed, that's when I become stronger and more determined. I try to do everything to the best of my ability.

My career was in hairdressing and fashion, and I had two very successful businesses, both brought forward, not from luck, but from sheer hard work and determination. My work ethic I attribute to both my parents.

I consider myself to be a good friend, I am kind and supportive if needed, and I am very loyal, I am honest to a fault and I am a planner by nature, and I love an itinerary. I know my shortcomings and I never blame anyone else for my failings. I believe totally in humility, humanity and honesty.

My true philosophy in life, is that there is a price to pay for everything, nothing in this life is free, I consider that I have worked for everything I have ever had, so I feel I have no price to pay, however, this does not mean that fate will not hand you a raw deal sometimes, but I am also a great fatalist who believes that bad times will also pass, nothing stays the same for ever. I do not believe in religion, and I make no apologies for this, I attribute this to the Catholic Religion and my life experiences. I now know for sure, that many of the above strengths I compliment myself on, are the reason I can make this journey with my husband and help him to reach the summit he so needs to reach

.

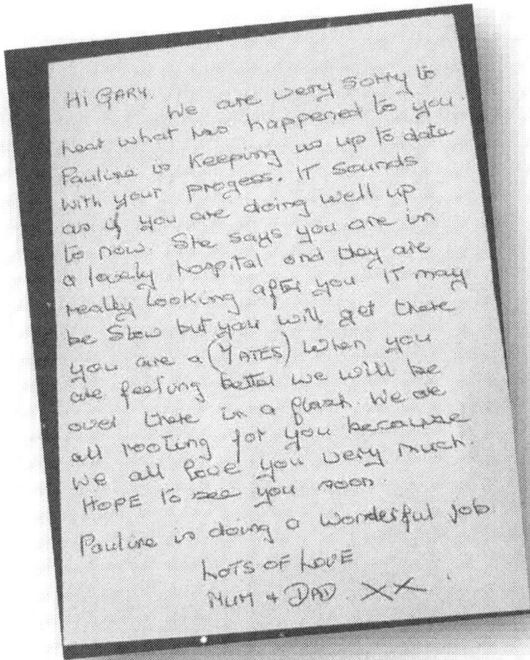

Hi GARY.
We are very sorry to
hear what has happened to you.
Pauline is keeping us up to date
with your progess. IT sounds
as if you are doing well up
to now. She says you are in
a lovely hospital and they are
really looking after you. IT may
be slow but you will get there
you are a (YATES) when you
are feeling better we will be
over there in a flash. We are
all rooting for you because
we all love you very much.
HOPE to see you soon.
Pauline is doing a wonderful job.
LOTS OF LOVE
MUM + DAD. XX

DAY TEN

As we walk along this steep, rocky path,
each gate we open and step through,
we will close behind us and never open it again.
But each gate takes us nearer to our destination,
where family and friends are waiting to welcome us.

The Stroke

I am in awe that ten days have passed since this horror started and we were in Spain, it seems like a lifetime ago, yet, it's gone in a heartbeat. Our lives have changed, unrecognisably in that time, I have no idea when we will see our friends and family again, I have no idea when normal life will ever arrive, but what I do know is, that our true friends will be a part of this life changing event, those who want to support us will be welcome on this journey, and we will be forever grateful for their unique part of things to come.

My thoughts venture to what will happen once we are at the Rehab Clinic, I intend to ask them if I can spend time at the clinic, to sit in on therapies, so I have an understanding and can help him on a daily basis. I have no commitments here in Switzerland, my work is finished for the foreseeable future, so time will be a commodity I have lots of.

I also have to sort out so much paperwork and Gary's financial affairs, there are the everyday things to deal with, things I have never been involved with as I have never lived here full time, my time has been spent between UK, Spain and Switzerland, we both dealt with our own affairs. That will now change, I will be responsible for everything. I have so many people to notify and so much to find out about payment of bills etc. Little did I know at this point, just how difficult a time this would prove to be, on top of everything else.

I will spend every night alone at the flat, and I am not very good at having too much time on my hands, I am used to being busy, so I don't know how that will work, time will tell.

I have no friends or network of support here, in fact I don't know anyone personal, no one to have a coffee with or help me with the language. I feel daunted suddenly, then I have to check myself and do what I do, tell myself to stop thinking too much about what I have to do later, and get on with what needs doing now.

A very tormented night for both of us, we cling to each other for support, there are tears, but we have both learnt to leave them there in the night. Worry, anxiety and fear are tumbling all around us, fear of the unknown. Worry about Gary being alone all night, how will he deal with being apart at such a vulnerable time, I have crucifying feelings about it, he can't talk, how will he cope with communicating to them, how will he get through the nights.

The Stroke

The sickness I feel inside is overwhelming, trying to overcome my dread but seeing his also. He seems so broken again, I feel so screwed up inside, my heart is pounding all the time, this has to be faced, I need to get control of my feelings, this is no time to be lost, no time to be stumbling around, I need to get my direction and save my energy for the real trip ahead.

I wonder if either of us is ready to leave this safe haven. We have had little sleep, I wonder if I will ever sleep thought free again, it's ten days since I slept in my own bed, ten days since I didn't feel worried, ten days since I felt normal, and ten days since I didn't feel sad inside.

02.00 hour. We sit on our respective chairs, there is no sleep forthcoming, so we drink tea, chat, go for a night-time walk around the corridors, have a whispered chat to the night staff, generally pass the time as we do at night. I keep wondering what will happen when I am not there with him when he can't sleep, I try to push the thoughts to one side for now, I practice what I preach, don't worry about things in the future that may never happen, easy to say hard to do, but that's what I do.

05.30, and we are getting ready, I have my shower first, then Gary. I have to pack our few belongings up and get ready for the doctor to come and see us. The sun is shining, and the day has begun for us, I feel calm now, and I need to make sure Gary is calm.

One of Gary's work colleagues is kindly coming to the hospital to take my car to the clinic for me so that I can travel with Gary, he is coming to the room to see Gary, first.

I explain that Vitali is coming, he looks bewildered really, I ask him if he knows who that is, and he shakes his head. I explain that it is someone who works at his Company, no more than that, and that he is taking the car to the clinic for us. He seems to accept this without drama.

When Vitali arrives at the room, I am nervous about it, not sure what to expect, but when Gary sees him, he looks unsure about how to react I think, but Vitali just takes the moment and makes it theirs. I walk him to the car, and he is gone. This is one big stress that been lifted off my shoulders, the car has been an ongoing stress to me from the onset. Having to keep moving it about but needing it near-by.

When I return to the room, I chat about how good it was of Vitali to do this for us, and how nice it was to see him, there is no response from

Gary, so I ask him if he remembers Vitali from work, he says no! I wasn't expecting that, Vitali is part of his team, they work closely together. I start to wonder who he does remember, so decide that once he is settled at the Rehab clinic I will check with photographs on my phone, feeling sure he will remember most people.

It is a busy morning, lots of form filling and signatures, checks performed on Gary, tubes removed, his arm looks very bruised, but it will heal. He seems so vulnerable again, unsure of what is going on, I feel all screwed up inside, my heart is racing, I have yet to explain to him that I can't stay overnight with him at the clinic, I have crucifying feelings inside about this it's so overwhelming trying to overcome my dread.

I am so nervous about telling him, I have no idea how he will take this news, and not sure when the right time is, I decide to leave it till we are there. I console myself with the fact that this is not my decision, it is out of my hands, and also, they will see what he is like at night and I feel sure they will come up with a solution, well that's what I hang on to.

Suddenly I remember it is only ten days since that fateful moment in Benidorm, it seems a lifetime away, really, how can it only be ten days, we have made a flight from Spain to Switzerland, he is heading for his fourth venue, life has been anything but normal for me, but we have survived so far.

The time arrives, we have said all our goodbyes during the morning, and we know we will probably never see this team again, we are moving on to meet our new team. Everything is packed and we are ready to go.

Our private ambulance car arrives. and this phase is finished, forty- five minutes later we arrive at Zihlschlacht Reha Klinic.

My first impression as we turn into the driveway, is one of a wonder at the beautiful surroundings, the grounds are just breath-taking for a clinic, more like the grounds of a hotel. It has views of majestic mountains covered in snow, what a joy I feel for Gary.

We are met at reception by such a warm and friendly lady, she gets us to sit in a small comfortable reception lounge and she proceeds to explain what will happen next. It does not seem at all like entering a clinic, no red tape, no officialdom, just smiling faces and easy conversation. It's hard to explain how I felt, but I was so happy to be at this next camp.

The Stroke

Gary in the wheelchair and me trotting behind, we are taken to his room, yet again I can't help but observe how immaculate everywhere is, there are beautiful flower arrangements in the public areas, there is such an air of ease here, it's palpable. Everyone we pass on our way, smiles at us and says hello, just like they have met us before. Little did I know at this point what a special lady our escort Rosa Marie would become to us.

We arrive at his room, this will be his home now for however long it takes, it's strange for me to think about going home alone, leaving him here, he is so vulnerable but I have to trust now in this team gathering around him and keeping him safe.

The room is just lovely, clean, bright, with a window letting in the sunshine, he has everything he needs with his own bathroom, everything is adapted to make sure he is safe and as independent with his daily needs as he can be. A larger than life male nurse arrives, he does not speak fluent English but we get along just fine, he explains as best as he can what we need to know at this time, and he seems fun, He puts Gary at ease for now, and I am very grateful for that. He tells me that the doctor will be here to see us shortly, and asks if we would like a coffee, which he duly brings.

It is not long before the doctor arrives, she looks young, but I quickly remind myself that yet again, that is because I am getting older! We shake hands, which, in Switzerland is the normal thing to do when meeting people in this type of situation, I am to find out as time goes on, that it doesn't matter how many times you meet up with the same person in a day, you will shake hands every time. It's a sign of respect for each other I assume, and a nice gesture I find.

So, it is time for all the questions now, and for her to familiarise herself with just where Gary is at this point. She has, of course, read all his notes, but still has lots of questions to ask me, she also directs questions at Gary, some he doesn't seem to understand others he shakes or nods his head. Although she makes lots of notes, she is very intent on watching him, just as I am very intent on watching her, I can see she looks into his eyes a lot, she speaks to him not at him, he will appreciate this.

Next, she says she would like to see if Gary can stand, so I offer, yes and he can walk also, she looks at me. She looks at her notes like she is trying to gather her thoughts, then says when did Mr Yates have his stroke again, I say November the 2nd. She actually looks at me as though she doesn't really believe me. She takes Gary's arm and asks him to stand. He does and she asks him to walk, which he does. She smiles and makes more notes, and says he is doing very well after such a short time. I virtually pat myself on the back and give Gary a huge smile.

She asks if I have any questions so far. The coward I am at this time, I use this opportunity to let Gary know I will not be able to stay with him overnight. I say to her I am very nervous about leaving Gary at night, and that I have been with him constantly since the stroke, and he has needed a lot of support during the nights. I explain that his mind works overtime, and he has very dark thoughts and is grieving for his past life, making it impossible for him to sleep, I also explain that he gets some sleep during the day. She looks very understanding and says this is normal and all this will be addressed and try not to worry about him too much.

She leaves us now and says I can stay till Gary is ready for bed, asking me to be back here in the morning for 09.00, and Gary will be safe and looked after. I believe her but I am starting to stress a little and have palpitations, I am also concerned about how many of the staff here speak English, or even in fact, any of the patients, of course I am fully aware that it will be predominantly Swiss patients.

We are alone now, and it's time to face the truth of my pending departure for the night, we look at each other, and very large pools of water fill Gary's eyes and I quickly wipe them away, before they can run down his face.

I start talking and telling him that this is the way it has to be, and we have to run with it for now. I am only a thirty- minute drive away, and this is his best chance of recovery. I also take the stand of emotional blackmail, telling him that I need to keep my strength up by getting more sleep, and I also need to attend to the flat and so many other pending details. This does the trick he gives me a watery smile and we hug each other tightly. I chat about bringing clothes for him tomorrow, and his toiletries. Ask him what else he needs; he just shakes his head.

The male nurse arrives again, bringing everything Gary will need, he is very chatty and he tries to put Gary at ease, I suppose he is so used to this, therefore he is the best person to do so, I am glad to have the distraction for us, he tells me in his own way that Gary will be just fine as he will be looking after him.

By 18.00 Gary is exhausted and I ask if he wants to get into bed, he nods, he really looks tired now, and I hope that maybe he will get some sleep. Before he has time to get into bed a nurse arrives. She shows Gary the call button next to his bed and tells him if he needs anything at anytime he just has to press it, and someone will come. There is so much I want to say to her, but I know there is no point, they will find out soon enough, and anyway she does not speak sufficient English to have a proper conversation. So, I console myself that they have been doing this for many patients for a long time and they must be good at it, as it's the best clinic in Switzerland, possibly in Europe.

I sit for a while, but I feel fatigue taking over and an intense feeling of tiredness. Gary is ready to doze I think, so I tell him it is time for me to leave, the look of sadness on his face, is one I never want to see again, but I am sure it will be a long time before this happens again. I stand and just wonder how I will get my legs to walk out of this place. I tell myself this is just the settling in the camp period for him, and he has everything he needs here,
everything that I can't provide for his recovery, a whole team of people to guide him along this unchartered path.

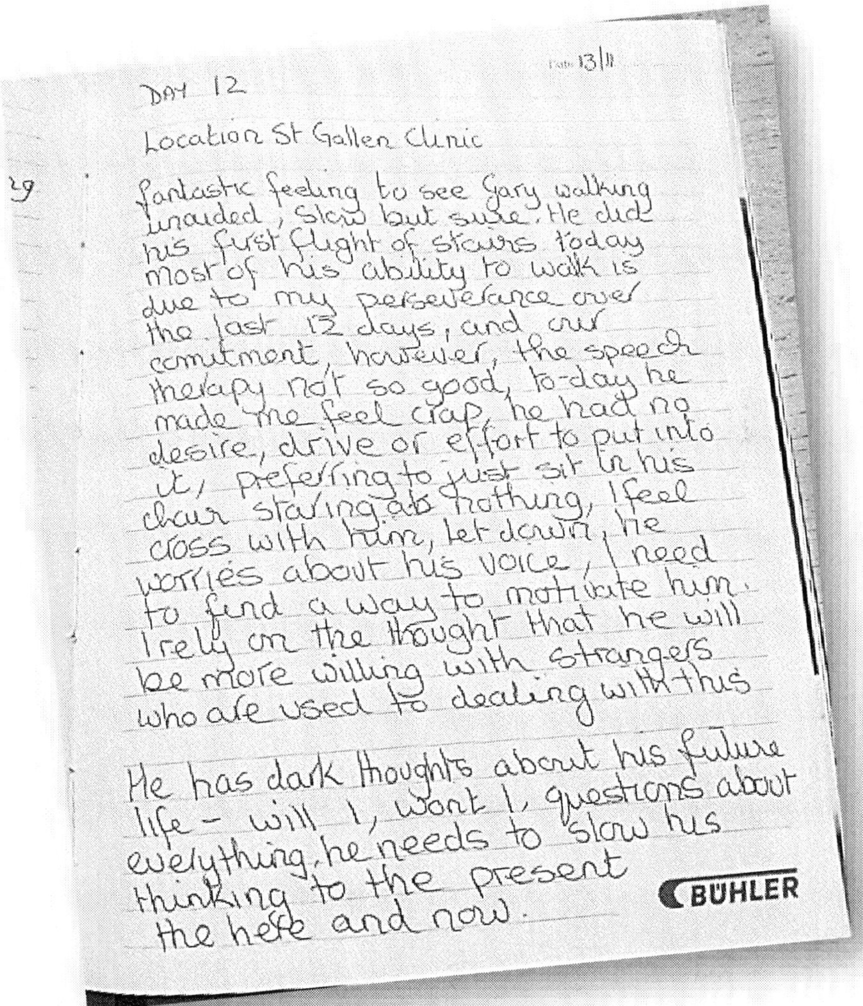

Date 13/11

DAY 12

Location St Gallen Clinic

29 fantastic feeling to see Gary walking unaided, slow but sure. He did his first flight of stairs today most of his ability to walk is due to my perseverance over the last 12 days, and our commitment, however, the speech therapy not so good, to-day he made me feel crap, he had no desire, drive or effort to put into it, preferring to just sit in his chair staring at nothing, I feel cross with him, let down, he worries about his voice, I need to find a way to motivate him. I rely on the thought that he will be more willing with strangers who are used to dealing with this

He has dark thoughts about his future life - will I, wont I, questions about everything, he needs to slow his thinking to the present the here and now.

OUR NEW PHASE

CHAPTER ONE

The Diary Continues

Every-thing is relaxed and calm around our new campfire.
We are at the base of our first real mountain ready to start the climb.
The sun is shining, and the experts are standing by to guide the way.
It's not the tough climb we are thinking about.
It's the view from the top we are looking forward to seeing.

This is the first time I have been alone for the last ten days, the first time I will be on my own at night, the first time I will be alone with my thoughts, I do not relish the deliberation of it at all. Even the walk down the corridor from Gary's room feels so lonely, I look around and realise I have no idea how to get out of this place, and I need to find the car-park and then my car, I have to ask at reception, so difficult with the language barrier, I make a mental note that I must make a concerted effort to learn this language, it's just too difficult in this situation not to.

It's dark and cold, my coat is not warm enough, but I have warm ones at the flat, the car park is over the road, it's deserted and I start to feel nervous, then I check myself, this is Switzerland, one of the safest places. I find the car with the aid of the alarm fob.

I can't remember the last time I ever felt so weary and alone, my footsteps feel heavy and my heart feels heavier, the car is cold, I am shivering, but I think that is due part to the tiredness, I am not looking forward to the drive, I need to sharpen my concentration, the roads are very winding on the entire journey. It's the longest half an hour drive ever, it's excruciatingly slow to me, I dare not have it too warm for fear of it making me feel even more tired.

I park the car in the garage, then I have to wonder how I will make it up the six flights of stairs, no lift in our apartment block, I have always hated these stairs and now is no exception. Half way up, I think about Gary, and how I will be able to get him up to the flat, suddenly this is a disturbing thought, he certainly would not be able to do this now and I fear not for a very long time, this means he will not be able to come home at weekends even if it is allowed.

The Stroke

He won't be able to come back to his own flat, this is not a good thing at all, and I immediately realise this will have to be addressed, and sooner rather than later. I dismiss this thought as best as I can, it is no use worrying about it now, I have to think about this later.

The flat is so quiet, a strange echoing quiet, but it is warm, I am grateful for that, but this is the only comfort, of course, there is no food or even milk, nothing for me to eat, I check the fridge but of course Gary cleared it out before he made his trip to Spain for the two weeks, however there is a bottle of wine, and suddenly I am thankful for small mercies, I feel in great need of that wine.

I open the wine, put the TV on and settle down to try to relax, but I can't, it's impossible to, I start to think about Gary, I am feeling so unsettled, I am having trouble even sitting, I want to pace about, I need to distract myself and the TV is not doing it.

I start to feel myself screaming inside, I can't stop it, I feel sick with concern for Gary, how will he deal with the night terrors alone. It's bad enough me dealing with mine, and I have no distraction myself, but poor Gary, I cannot bear the thought of him suffering alone through the night, but what can I do, nothing at all. I have to trust that the nursing staff will have all the tools and experience to make this right for him, I am worried also that he will try to get out of bed on his own, but I can't be there, and I tell myself he is not the first person with this stroke and his associated problems that they have looked after and kept safe.

I need to talk to someone, so I call my longest standing friend Kate, she knows me better than anyone, I know she will tell me to man up, and if I cry she will tell me to stop that nonsense, and that's just what I need right now.

She is as predicted, supportive but firm, kind but tough, she is impressed that I have wine and tells me that's just what I need, we chat and I start to feel a little better, well at least a lot calmer. I know she is having to put a brave face on, but that's what we always do for each other, she offers to fly out to Switzerland from the UK and come and stay with me, but I am way too concerned about her making the six flights of stairs on any sort of regular basis as she has Asthma, and would struggle too much. I say I can't have anyone else to worry about or look after, I get a few expletives from her but we both laugh, she says she would manage it, but it's early days yet for these decisions, I need to see how things go with Gary settling in.

I have a phone call with Jackie after Kate's call, and she is just as calming for me, I just bring her up to date with the day's happening's and tell her about the clinic. Neither Kate or Jackie at any point of our conversations say those words I couldn't take at the moment, "don't worry everything will be ok", and I am very grateful to them for their sensitivity. Anyone who says this to me, in the near future, will be at the threat of getting both barrels, there is nothing going to be ok about this for a very long time, I am a realist and one thing I am certain of, is that this is a very serious situation for Gary, his brain is severely injured, at this point I still don't have all the facts and don't know what his recovery prognosis is, that's if they can even predict it at this point, which I don't believe they can.

Although it has only been ten days, I have faced a lot of facts and demons, I have accepted my life has changed and that Gary is my priority, whatever that means, if I have to put my life on hold, then that's the way it will be. This is the very time that you must put the other person before yourself, if you can't do this for them, then it is going to be a very tough and bumpy journey for both.

The sooner anyone who is faced with this situation, accepts that their life as they know it is over for now, nothing will be normal, and everything will be difficult, the sooner they will understand the journey they are on.

I have accepted my challenge, I have taken the mantle in both hands, my husband needs me like he has never needed me before and he deserves to have me by his side, I am just showing him the loyalty and love that I know he would show me. This is not the time to be self-absorbed or selfish, to be self- pitying and recriminating, this is the time to offer your strength and love to the one person that should deserve it, Gary does deserve it. My life is his for now, and I gladly give it to him.

I have the TV on quite loud, although I am not watching it, but I need the noise in the back ground, my wine is going down a treat and I feel somewhat relaxed, but at the same time I still have anxiety, but who would expect anything else.

The Stroke

I have decided to put a status on Facebook, I tell everyone that I will only be putting positive updates on here, and I will be glad to hear from everyone who wants to respond. There will be no negativity on the page from now, and I thank everyone again for their support on social media and their good wishes, I feel that and as I have said before Facebook will be a great way for me to stay in contact with everyone, and I will not be under pressure to try to contact individual people for now. There are so many lovely messages, even from people in our Spanish village that we hardly know, people coming together for us from afar.

It gets late, but I can't face getting into bed, I know I won't sleep, even as tired as I am, I do not want to lie in bed restlessly trying to force sleep onto myself, which I know will be impossible, so I decide to bring the quilt and pillow to the settee, I will be much more comfortable, and I can try to concentrate on a film maybe. The night passes slowly, but I am resting. I tell myself that there will come a time, soon I hope, that we will both accept the situation and we will both be comfortable with it, this has to be or we won't be able to survive.

The dawn arrives with rays of sunshine, I gather my quilt around me and go to sit on the balcony, no reason for this, I just felt like doing it, it's cold but sunny, and I feel more at peace today. It's early, so I decide on my timings for getting to the clinic for 09.00. I need to stop on the way to get a coffee and maybe a croissant, my stomach feels like an empty tin box, I feel hungry, a good sign, I think.

I pack some things for Gary, then shower, and get ready, I wear something nice and apply my makeup and do my hair, I figure that if I look normal, like Gary would be used to seeing me, then he will see more confidence in me, those are my thoughts and I am happy with them.

Although I didn't sleep during the night, once I am ready, I feel remarkably refreshed, I was comfortable, so my body feels rested, again, I remind myself how important it is to be able to relax and rest my own body. I could be carrying a very heavy rucksack with all our equipment on this journey ahead!

Driving through beautiful countryside with the sun shining makes the journey very easy, I have always been in awe of the stunning scenery here in Switzerland and this thirty- minute drive is no exception with its breath-taking views. The lack of traffic makes it relaxing and pleasant. I am happy to be feeling some normality to my thoughts. I stop at the petrol station and pick up a coffee and croissant and I am amazed at how much I am looking forward to it. I smile at how those little things can please so much sometimes.

The journey is exactly thirty minutes, I feel grateful that it is so close, it would have been so much more difficult to have to take a longer journey each time. I arrive and park the car then walk to the clinic, I take a couple of wrong turns as yet again I have no idea where to go, as many people already know I have no sense of direction whatsoever, but I eventually arrive at reception, I will not even attempt to find his room, that would be a non -starter and would result in me wandering the corridors aimlessly, I couldn't even remember which floor he was on, so I ask at reception, miraculously, the guy spoke fairly good English and directed me.

As I made my way towards Gary, I felt quite confident and although I had a few jitters I was just looking forward to seeing him and reassuring him I am here with him, and still supporting him all the way. Also, it is time for us to get more information as to what happens now. People smiled and said hello whenever they passed, it feels so friendly and warm.

I could not have been prepared for what came next. I made my way down the corridor to Gary's room, the door was open and there was a bustle of activity in there, Gary was still in bed, and I was instantly asked to wait outside, it took me by surprise and I felt those old stomach churning feelings grabbing me again.

This is not how I expected this to go. I felt extremely anxious, after only a couple of minutes, a nurse appeared, she asked me to sit down, there was a small table and two chairs in the corridor opposite his room, I sat and I found myself staring at the vase of flowers on the table, unable to look at the nurse, why was this, I didn't know, she was talking and I was listening but couldn't look at her. She was asking me if I would like a coffee, I said I had just had one thanks. She said they were just getting Gary ready. I sensed something was wrong, that this did not seem like just getting him ready, was I overreacting, I must be. She also said that the doctor was going to talk to me once she had finished seeing Gary.

The Stroke

Well I knew I was seeing the doctor this morning so I suppose I should not read anything into that. She asked me to wait there again and went back into the room. I was now desperate to see him, and all my relaxed feelings had abandoned me and been replaced with the old anxiety and stress, why on earth did I think this was suddenly going to be easy. I wondered, why I thought everything would be lifted off of my shoulders because we had changed camps is a mystery to me at this moment.

Reality suddenly slams into me. Nothing has changed for Gary since yesterday, he hasn't gone home for the night, had wine and chatted to friends, on the phone, watched a spot of TV whilst relaxing on his own sofa under a quilt.

He hasn't driven in the sunshine enjoying the scenery and drinking a coffee with a croissant on the side, no, he has spent the night in a strange bed, in an unfamiliar room with strangers all around him, no sign of me anywhere when he wakes up. I am so close to tears, it is becoming difficult to hold them back, I just keep taking deep breaths, every time

I take a deep breath I can feel the oxygen rushing to my brain, I feel light headed, I am desperate to calm myself down, I am feeling such panic. For the second time since his stroke, I have been prevented from being with him, I am sitting in another sterile corridor, alone, unable to deal with my thoughts, trying to block them out, I don't know what to think, I just need to know what is happening.

After an unbearable wait, the doctor comes out, I stand and she introduces herself and shakes hands, as is the Swiss way. She asks me to sit down and she does the same, she looks so calm, and not worried or serious, so I guess that's a good sign.

I ask immediately if Gary is alright, she says quite openly, that he has had a bad night, my heart bleeds. She confirms what I already truthfully knew, that he was very upset in the night, and he didn't get any sleep, I explained that this happens every night, but I have been there to support him up to now, and I am very concerned about this.

She says the sleeping tablets will be changed, but also, he will now be given anti- depressants, she says this is routine after any stroke, but particularly after such a severe one. The doctor explains that this measure is to help relax him, she says it will help him to deal with things in a more positive way. She assures me that there will be a very positive change to him, and it will certainly help him to sleep.

I feel instant relief flooding over me. She tells me I can go into him now and she will be coming back at 11.00 to do some tests and to speak to us. She tells me to try not to worry, he is in the best place possible and they are here to support both him and me. I thank her and tell her I appreciate this and will see her later.

Once I get into the room, it clears quickly, Gary is dressed and sitting in the chair, I go to him and give him the biggest hug ever, we hold onto each other for long minutes, I am so happy to see him. When I pull back, he has the saddest eyes, he is struggling to hold back tears, but I know he is trying to be strong for me, he must be fully aware that this is the only option, the best option, he knows we have to do this. I hate seeing him like this, it's like taking our first steps on the mountain path but stumbling straight back down. I have to pull him back up and draw his strength out again, I need to see some light in his eyes, they are too dark.

I mentally make the decision that we will not spend unnecessary time in the room, it's just a bedroom essentially and that's what it should be treated as, we need to integrate into the surroundings, this is his home for now so he needs to familiarise himself with it. I tell him we will go and take a little walk around the clinic and find our way around.

On Gary's corridor there are six rooms for patients, a central office where the staff congregate, a small open sitting area with four chairs, a patient canteen, and a reception desk at the entrance.

As we pass by the reception desk, I am welcomed again by the lady who checked us in Rosa Maria, she comes out from behind the desk and asks if everything is alright, and do we need anything, I say yes all is good but could she tell us if there is anywhere that we can go for a coffee, she directs us to the coffee shop on the floor below, she tells me to just ask if we need anything at all.

We take the lift down and find it easily. It is just like a regular coffee shop, and has lovely views of the grounds outside, I let Gary choose a table, and in a very short time we make this our regular table, very typically English I later comment. I put on an upbeat manner and order two coffees, the staff behind the counter are really friendly and one speaks good English, so that is very confidence building at this point and boy do I need something positive.

I feel very nervous about addressing Gary's first night experience, but I have never shied away from facts and truth, and I think it is important for me to acknowledge that he had a bad night. I ask him lots of questions, knowing the answer to all of them anyway, the answers are as expected, he did of course have the same dark thoughts but this time he didn't have me to comfort him. I tell him about my conversation with the doctor, and that I feel confident that they will be able to help him to sleep better, I say that the doctor did not seem at all surprised and she said this was perfectly normal and it would be sorted. I hope this make him feel somewhat better, but I know I am reaching for the stars at this moment. But all I can do is try.

As we sit enjoying our coffee, I ask him further questions, did he have breakfast, a nod, did he have it in his room, again a nod, has he had a shower, he nods yes again. Next I start to tell him about my evening, that I had spoken to Kate and Jackie, and that I didn't go to bed as I felt lonely without him, so I had slept on the sofa, he smiled at this, and I said, the bed is just too big without him, again he smiles. Making him smile over the next few months will become my quest for every day. I have always been able to make him laugh, even by text, so that has to continue. I review my drive to the clinic, telling him there is little traffic and stunning views, and it is a really pleasant drive, so he need not worry about me.

I discuss with him that I will need to use his Debit card for money, petrol food etc. I remind him that I have his pin number, until I can sort something else out, he shakes his head and waves the air away, I know he is telling me to just use his card. I have no idea at this point, what a nightmare will ensue, where the finances are concerned.

We pass the time away, me chatting about anything I can think of, it's not easy when everything is just a one -way conversation, and I can't bear heavy silences at the moment, I need to fill our minds.

During our time in the coffee shop, many people come and go, some patients on their own and some with family or friends. But it is so disturbing to see so many people who have had strokes, and I am shocked to see how many young people, for sure there are some who have had even more severe strokes than Gary.

The Stroke

At least Gary can walk, even though it is a struggle for him, so many are in wheelchairs with severe paralysis, I start to wonder how long some of them have been here, and of course how long Gary will be here. I suppose it's like asking how long a piece of string is. We just have to wait and see and hope he responds to his therapy, I decide to park that thought right here, and not think about things that cannot be answered right now, too soon for looking for an exit date.

It's time to return to the room in readiness for the doctor. True to form, I can't remember the way, and to my great surprise Gary has no problem, he leads us straight back, it takes me back a bit, and I am full of praise for him. We take our seats at the little table opposite the room and sit nervously waiting.

When the time comes, a team of four people arrive, and we are taken back into the room. Everyone shakes hands and introduces themselves, I know I will not remember anyone's name after they have left, or in fact after they have told me. I was not wrong. I put a calm exterior on over a not so calm interior. Gary looks perfectly calm and I feel happy for this.

I hear the same things I have already heard many times, like, severe stroke, large injury to the brain, paralysis, etc etc etc. I just listen without comment. They ask me questions about what happened at the time of the stroke, so I live it over again, Gary has no recollection of the day whatsoever, coping mechanism I call it. The head doctor tells us that she has read all his notes and seen all the scans, but they will be doing a scan themselves tomorrow, I am happy about this.

Without preparation or warning the doctor produces some cards from her pocket, each card has four objects on it, Key, Door, Pen, Dog, for instance, everyday objects, she shows Gary a card and asks him to point to the key, Gary looks and I can see he is concentrating intently, looking from one item to another, then he just looks at the doctor and shakes his head. If I could describe what I think my face looked like at that moment I would have to say, disbelief, bewilderment and shock.

She shows no surprise and says that's great Mr Yates. She looks at my face and of course she can see my reaction, so she tells me not to worry, that Gary has Aphasia, at this point I had never heard of this, I ask her what it is and she says, it affects the cognitive skills. I have my next online research to do tonight, that should fill my evening nicely. They do reflex tests and a myriad of other tests.

She explains that he will have a programme of therapies every day, which will start tomorrow. I ask her if the therapists speak English as Gary does not speak German, she tells me she is aware of this and they will make sure that this is covered. There will be an auxiliary who will come to pick him up and escort him there and back for every therapy, so not to worry about finding the rooms. She adds that I am welcome to join him at his first therapies if I wish, I say I would like to do that. She explains to him that he will have help getting ready in the morning and again at bedtime, but they will be helping him to be as independent as possible. She shows me his itinerary, my first thought is, 'Holy Crap,' how will he get through those every day. Next she gives me a menu list for the week and asks if I can please fill it in for him, I think 'Holy Crap' again, as to my horror, it is all in German. I hope that my experiences in Austrian restaurants when skiing, will stand me in good stead for this task, otherwise he could be in big trouble.

She thinks this is enough information for now and I wholeheartedly agree. We shake hands and they move on. As soon as they are gone, and I think I have time to unpack for Gary, a nurse arrives, introduces herself and shakes hands, I don't think I need to mention this every day every person process again. The nurse is so nice, she tells us everything he needs to know about his meal time, she also adds that if I want to eat in the restaurant, I can notify them and Gary's meal will be brought down for him, then we can eat together, this sounds perfect to us. I have been worried about how he will be able to make friends or integrate properly, not just because of this lack of speech but also his lack of understanding of the language, I have a dread of him sitting on his own, spending too much time in his room when I am not here. It is a strange world for him, and I really don't know at this point how this will work. But completely accept in my mind that these people are specialists in dealing with stroke victims, and they will be aware of all my doubts and concerns.

I feel the need to ask about his sleeping pattern, and how they can help him, she says he has already been started on different sleeping tablets and his anti- depressants, and they will kick in very fast, this is great news for me and I feel very confident about it. Let's hope my new confidence is founded.

The nurse goes through the workings of the room, he has a call button that he must use at night if he needs to get out of bed for anything including the toilet, although he is still wearing a catheter at night, I also doubt that he understands what she is saying, she explains the tv remote, but that's a non-starter as there are no English channels, I make a mental note to bring his iPad and teach him how to use it, at least for watching some football maybe, when he first gets into bed, it should help relax him.

The nurse tells us it is nearly time for dinner and would we like to eat together in the restaurant, only patients are allowed in the patients eating area, I say yes and she says we should go to the restaurant now so I can order my food and Gary's will be brought down.

We make our way to the restaurant, which Gary remembers the route again, I do not, and we take the same table, as we will now for every trip here. I check out the menu and recognise quite a lot of the food, so I place my order, nice and simple. We have an apple juice to drink and settle down to what I hope is a nice meal and of course one that Gary will eat and enjoy, even though he is still on soft food, I hope it is presented as well as the Hospital food was.

The restaurant starts to fill up, other patients with family or friends dining together, no one takes any notice of us, a lot of people in wheelchairs or on crutches, so many very poorly people, I look at Gary and see how perfect he looks sitting opposite me, he doesn't look ill like these people, if anyone just looked at him sitting here they would not think there was anything wrong with him, it's only when he stands to walk that it becomes apparent, or you realise that his arm just hangs by his side, I feel that sadness creeping over me again.

After a very nice dinner, good quality and well cooked, and Gary's presented really nice, he ate well considering. We make our way back to his floor, we settle down at the table in the corridor, it's very quiet and I wonder what we can do, I need to think about our relaxation time and occupy us, maybe I will see if Gary can play cards, I will bring them tomorrow and see. We are only sitting a few minutes when a nurse arrives to take Gary's blood pressure, this will be regular thing throughout the day, blood pressure is a very important check after a stroke I am to learn.

Everything is fine. After she has done that she asks us if we would like coffee, which she duly brings and it's so nice to feel looked after.

People seem to finish their meals and retire to their respective rooms, at 19.00 hrs, I see that Gary is tired, I ask him if he would like to go to bed and he nods yes, we return to his room and he gets ready for bed, during this time the nurse returns with his medication, she points to his notice board and there, is his therapy programme for the week and a copy for me, very thoughtful I think to myself.

With Gary comfortable in bed, I sit with him for a while and talk to him about feeling safe, and trying not to focus on negative stuff, I talk to him about making plans for the future and tell him to remember that our life has not stopped and we will still be able to go to our home in Spain again one day, things are just on hold for now, I talk about how lucky I feel to still have him and how different it could have been, I tell him that the alternative is unthinkable and that having him with me is the most important thing, and what does he think my life would be without him.

It is time for me to leave, again it is very hard to walk out of that clinic alone, I wonder again how he will be during the night, but I know I have to let this go, I have to trust the decision we have made and trust it is the right one. If I can't get some peace about leaving him then I will never get peace in myself, and truthfully, I need to get some rest both for my body and my mind.

For my drive home I put the music on loud, and take it slowly, trying to clear my mind, I stop to pick up something to eat and decide I must get some normality in my time at the flat, this is now my home for a long time and I have to feel comfortable and be able to relax there. These are positive thoughts and I start making a mental list of things I need to prioritise quickly, so that I minimise problems later. I will put that list onto paper tonight, and free up my mind. Writing things down has always worked for me and this is my plan.

Parking the car in the garage brings the dread of the quiet flat to me, I have always been very comfortable in my own company and space, but this place has never really been my home, just a place I visited during the Winter, where-as, Summers were much nicer when we spent weekends and holidays together in Spain, lots of friends and nice things to do, we never had a social life here and no time to make friends. Weekends we went skiing and when as Gary was at work during the week, I just spent my time mostly bored during the day, my highlight being planning and cooking nice dinners for us. I had a routine, I would drop Gary off at work for 07.00 then stop in the village for a coffee and croissant for breakfast, return the car then walk back down for the ingredients for dinner. Back to the flat and try to amuse myself, laundry and cleaning are of course part of that, until Gary sends a message for me to pick him up, it's the brightness to my day when he appears with a big smile on his face. He works hard so in the evening we enjoy our meal, relax and chat. We look forward to the weekends and our drive to various resorts, generally in Austria to ski. We love to ski and it's always a great fun time together, which makes up for the weekday's monotony for me. So that has been Switzerland for me until now, it's a whole new ball game for now, and one I have to get used to.

The Stroke

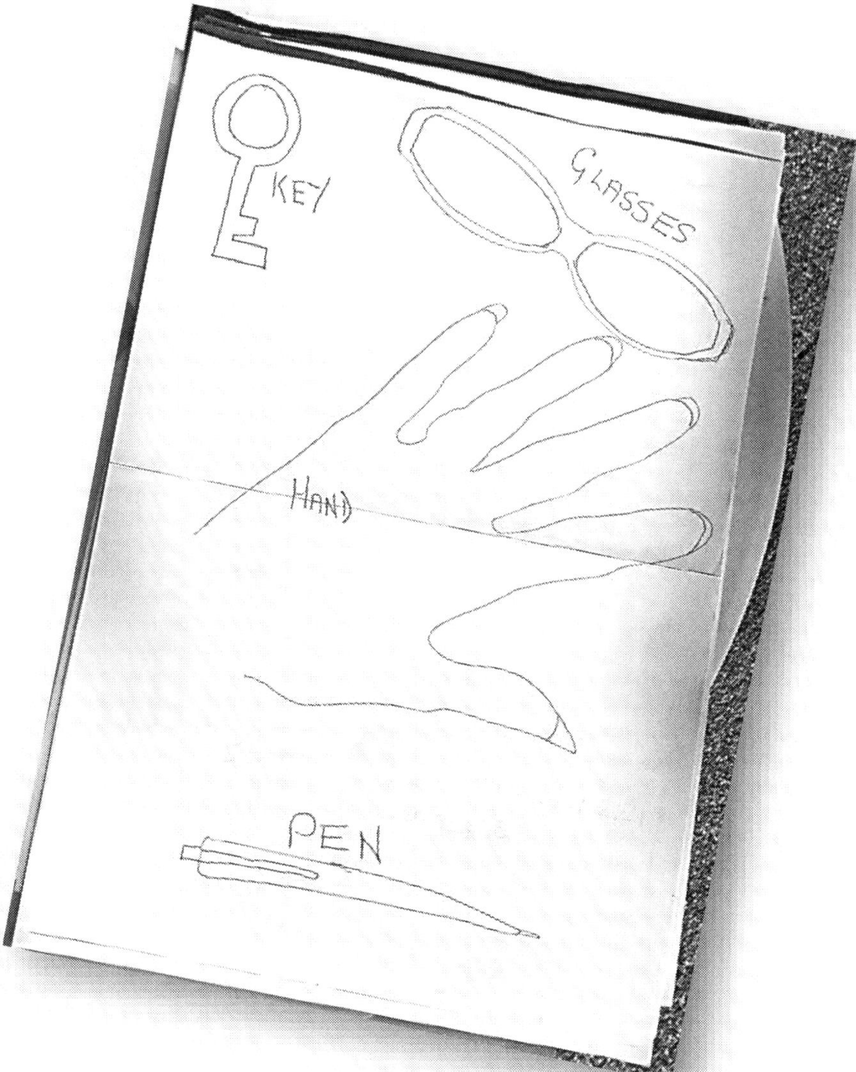

CHAPTER TWO

Don't underestimate life,
Every day counts.
make every moment special.
Look back on every day,
and know that you succeeded.

I arrive at the clinic at 08.30, seems early but his first therapy is at 09.00 and I want to make sure I am not late or flustered. When I reach the floor, he is in the food hall finishing breakfast, he looks very happy to see me, but also, he looks a lot happier in general, I dare to think that maybe he had a good night. I gesture for him to carry on, but he struggles out of his chair and comes over to give me a kiss, I tell him to finish his breakfast and I will sit here in the corridor and wait. A nurse spots me and immediately offers me coffee, which I very eagerly accept. My whole being is a little in shock, I feel a great pressure lifted suddenly from me.

Once he has finished, we slowly walk back to what becomes our table in the corridor and wait. At 08.45 an auxiliary lady arrives to take us to his first therapy, these first therapies will be assessments, and decisions on which therapy is best, will be made after they review the results. We sit and wait in another corridor along with other patients, everyone keeps themselves to themselves, but this is the Swiss way. In my experience, unless they know you, they seem to be very insular people. The five years Gary has been at the flat here, he doesn't know anyone, and although I used to pass people on the stairs, no one acknowledged me, even in the street in the village, no one makes eye contact with you, and for an English person that is very strange.

The Therapist arrives, introduces herself and we are led into her room. I take a seat at the back of the room, I do not want to interfere in any way, I just want to observe and hopefully be able to learn how to support Gary in his learning process. His first therapy is Speech, apparently, she needs to assess his Aphasia. He spends forty- five minutes in therapy then he has a thirty minutes break, so we go to the coffee shop for a coffee, our table is waiting. Once the lady brings the coffee, she asks me if we will be eating in the restaurant together again tonight and I say yes, she says she will notify them upstairs, I momentarily wonder how she remembered us after only once eating there, then consider how most of the Swiss dress, and accept that I am somewhat memorable here with how I dress, and I wear make-up and always do my hair nice, so I suppose it's not that surprising, but I still think it is very nice to ask us.

Back to the corridor and we are collected again and taken to another area and another therapist. Lunchtime arrives and again we eat in the restaurant, after lunch Gary goes to his room and has a rest, he is tired, this is a lot for him suddenly. I leave him to rest and take up my position at our table, I have my diary to bring up to date and a few calls to make, during this time I am offered a cup of coffee, and I am to learn very quickly that this will be the normal, and I am often very grateful for it.

The staff, from the receptionists, nurses, auxiliaries and through to the doctors are very friendly, respectful and helpful. Not too many of them speak much English, but most speak a little and with my basic German we manage very well. I spend forty-five minutes quite relaxed for the first time in what feels like forever, I dare to hope that Gary will settle in well and we can start his recovery in earnest. To have the support of such a large team of people is like hope has entered my heart. Gary has other people who will be responsible for him not just me, this will surely be a huge confidence builder for us both.

The day passes very fast, from one therapy to the next with coffee breaks in between, and a rest for Gary after lunch, this seems to be the norm for everyone, and spending time together just sitting at our table in the corridor and relaxing. But I realise soon enough that I need to fill some of this time, we can't just sit staring at each other for the time between therapies, but there is time to think about that once we know what results his assessments bring.

Nurses are busy doing the rounds of blood pressure check, medication handed out and generally making sure everyone is ok, some are more chatty than others, but I think that is because some speak better English of course. Most people go to their rooms after dinner and seem to stay there, everyone has a TV so maybe they just watch and relax, the days are very tiring for everyone, a stroke necessitates lots of rest. Gary now looks tired, it's 18.30 so I ask if he would like to go to bed now and he nods yes, with a bit of an apologetic look on his face, I smile and tell him not to be sorry, he needs his rest and I have to drive thirty minutes home and I also need my rest. I make myself look busy in his room and let him get himself ready for bed, noting that I will need to get him some new pyjamas etc, so I have time to wash them for him.

He is still having problems at night so it is essential I have clean changes for him until this is sorted, and I don't want to draw attention to it, as I know it is a constant source of upset to him, as it would be to anyone in his position. I am sure the nurses deal with it in a very professional and understanding way. I do keep reminding him that this is temporary and will be sorted at some stage, he needs to be reassured often. Once he is in bed, we chat for a while, I ask if he would like me to leave his phone he says no, he has no interest in his phone at all, so I can only surmise that he is not sure how to use it. I will not mention his phone again for now, I am sure the results of the assessments will give me a clearer picture of his capabilities at this point in time. After my usual pep talk, we say our goodnights, I remind him I will be back in the morning and it's time for me to make my lonely drive home.

On my journey home, I start to wonder questions like, how long will he stay at the clinic full time, how long before we see any positive results, but quickly realise that this is a waste of energy, so I put the music up loud and just try to have a relaxed drive.

It's hard to describe how I feel about going back to the flat, it's never been my home, it's very impersonal to me, it's very basic as it was furnished for ease of looking after, it's nice, but not home to me, so I almost feel as though I am going back to a temporary living space, however, I am fully aware that this will be my home for a long time maybe, so I decide I have to make it more homely for myself. It seems like a positive plan. Although I now know that Gary is safe and well looked after, I will not be leaving him to return to either England or Spain, unless I have to, and I hope that will not happen for any reason.

My mind turns to serious and important matters, I have to sort my residency out as soon as possible, it seems an impossible task at the moment as I have no idea where to start, but I decide that the Town Hall in the village must be a good starting point, I will address that, once this first week is over and I know what we are facing with Gary's recovery. This has to go first on my list, after that I have to go and notify the Bank of the situation and get them to advise me what I should do about his accounts, for now I can use his Debit card for cash and shopping, but I need to gain access, these are priority things to get sorted.

CHAPTER THREE

Someone said to me yesterday,
"I don't know how you find the strength,
to do this every day".
I replied, "I didn't find it, I always had it".

A new day, another drive to the Clinic and my takeaway coffee and croissant, this will be my daily breakfast now, but I do wonder what affect this will have on my waistline over time, but immediately decide to enjoy it now and worry about it later.

When I turn into the corridor to Gary's room, he is sitting at the table in the corridor, as soon as he sees me he gives me the biggest smile and rises from the chair to come to meet me, my heart soars and I feel happy to see him looking more like himself. There is a letter telling me that the Doctor will be coming later this morning at 11.00, and I know we will have further news about Gary's condition, part of me needs more information but a part of me is dreading it.

Gary has 2 therapies before he sees the doctor, so I sit in on them, and they are good to watch, I realise I can help him so much more if I know what they are doing together during the therapy time. I personally think it will be a great idea to try to take the therapies and match them to things in everyday life. Gary is a practical person, and this should help him with his understanding of things, well that's my hope for now.

We wait at our table for the doctor, she arrives and takes us into Gary's room. The report is very hard to take in all in one go, I know I have a thousand questions, but I really don't know where to start, she has given us the facts, so for now I have to digest them, then I will have a better idea of the things I need to ask her. It's a bit daunting to say the least.

Gary has long and short-term memory loss, the doctor suggests that I try to find out who and what he remembers, ok I think to myself, that's do-able, I have no idea at this point how shocking that will seem. He can't read, he has trouble differentiating between yes and no, his speech is severely affected. He cannot recognise objects on paper, he actually can't pick out an Elephant from a bed for example, it's that extreme.

The doctor gave an example, she asked him. Where is your leg? He just looked all around but had not a clue what that meant. There was a lot more involved at this meeting, but so much of it just washed over me, too much to take in and remember, later I am to think that maybe it's a bit of a coping mechanism to forget half the information for now. I need to think about the memory loss, address this first and see where it takes us. Our journey gets more interesting every day.

After the doctor leaves, it's time for lunch so we make our way to the restaurant and take our usual table. Whilst we are waiting for our food to arrive, I pick friends names out at random and ask him if he knows them, he doesn't recognise any of the names, I remember that he knew Artur when he visited us, so maybe he needs to see them not just hear the name, so I pick photographs at random and show him, including his own daughter and he didn't recognise them.

I show him a picture again of his daughter and say this is Holly, do you know who she is? He shakes his head. Well to say this was a blow is an understatement. Next I show him a picture of our home in Spain and ask him, if he knows where this is, again he has no idea, and shakes his head. He does not seem upset in the least about this which seems a little odd to me, but on the other hand it's good for him not to feel stress about it. My reading glasses are on the table, I ask him if he can pass them to me, he just looks around the table, then looks at me as if to say, what is that. I just smile and pick them up.

Now I know I need to speak to the doctor again before I take this any further, I'm not sure whether I should tell him who and what everything is straight away, or over a period time. Will he be upset when he realises, he should know these people? I need to check.

I wonder at how the brain processes things, does it process differently, how it sees a picture to how it processes the real object or real person, interesting thought, and one I will try to investigate. Surprisingly, I don't feel that worried about this aspect, I feel pretty certain that once Gary is faced with friends in the correct situation, he will recognise them, after all, he knows who I am, and knew me from the onset. This is not something I feel will create much of a negative to his life, certainly something we can deal with whatever the outcome.

We drift through the lunchbreak hour, I chatter on about what I have to sort out, we observe the other people in the restaurant, feeling sad that there are so many young people, and I mean young, a few look in their teens, its unthinkable to me that anyone so young would have a stroke, I feel very sad, not only for they themselves, but also for their parents, I can only begin to imagine how you would feel seeing your son or daughter struggling with life all of a sudden. I turn my attention to the Garden, I feel a need to get outside, to breathe some fresh air, it is unnaturally hot throughout the clinic, we walk around the grounds to get back to Gary's room, where he is now ready for a sleep.

My time now is spent researching how to apply for residency, so difficult as most sites are of course in Swiss language and Swiss is different to German. I come back to my original idea of going to the Town Hall, I will check on my way home, as to whether the opening times are on the outside of the building, then I can decide when to go, hoping of course that there is someone who speaks English.

The Bank I know opens at 08.00 hrs every weekday morning, so I will try to get an appointment early next week. I am amused now, at how naïve I was to think that this was going to be easy, I could not have been more wrong, this process turned out to be my worst nightmare at this point in the proceedings. As if I didn't have enough to think about and concentrate on, the Bank made things fifty times harder to deal with life.

It's one thing dealing with your partners stroke but doing it in a different Country brings extreme problems on many levels. Problems that you don't foresee coming. Most human beings expect people to have empathy and understanding towards you in this type of situation, when this does not happen, then your faith in human nature takes a battering.

Everything became so much harder for me over and above the clinic, and Gary's care. Ironically, Gary became the pleasure in my days, the joy in my eyes, watching him achieve small daily targets was my pleasure. The clinic became my sanctuary not just Gary's, a place where I could help him, and forget for a while each day, about the stress going on all around me.

The bank manager spoke excellent English which I thought was a great start, he seemed shocked at my news but remained professional and business like. I explained that I needed to take control of Gary's financial affairs and asked him what the best way to approach this was. I explained that I had no way of transferring my money as I had no accounts there and I was not a resident so could not open one yet. I told him I was ok to get cash and pay for daily needs as I knew the password for Gary's debit card. I also explained that I could not access Gary's online banking as he could not remember his passwords, and that meant I could not pay his online bills.

I had already contacted his credit card company to ask if they could send paper statements and I would then be able to pay them, but they said that due to Gary being paperless billing, he had to request statements from his account online, I reminded them again that I could not access his online account due to the password problem, and the guy said there is nothing we can do to help you. So, here started my nightmare. I explained all this to the Bank Manager, assuming he would realise the urgency of the matter.

He assured me that he would contact head office and get the forms sorted for me to sign and everything would be sorted very quickly. Adverse to this, two days later I filled the car up with petrol, tried to pay with the debit card and it was declined.

Ninety francs owing and no way to pay. I tried in vain to explain my predicament in some acceptable manner, but the attendant had no idea what I was saying. Very fortunately for me, another customer in the queue, who spoke English, very kindly came to my rescue, once the situation was explained, I was just asked to bring the money when I could, nothing more nothing less. This was the first time I realised how trusting Swiss people are, and just how honest they expect people to be. My nightmare continues to get worse.

I drove home, a sinking feeling in the pit of my stomach, my first thought, the Bank must have stopped the card. Back to the Bank tomorrow.

My next meeting was less than convivial, I told the manager what had happened, so he made a phone call and it was confirmed, the card had been cancelled. I reiterated again that I had no means of obtaining any money or paying bills, so what did they suggest I was going to do? He said that head office had written me a letter, and that would explain what needed to happen. Ok, I thought, this is just a glitch and will soon be sorted, after all, if Gary can't deal with his affairs, then as his wife, I have every right to do so. The Bank knows that, don't they?

It would be too lengthy to describe everything that I was put through by The Bank, but they put me through one of the most stressful periods I had to endure at this time, and it took almost five months before I could access the accounts. It necessitated in me having to fly to the UK, flying in one day, to collect cash, flying to Spain then next day, to get our marriage and birth certificates, and flying out the next day, leaving Gary at a very vulnerable time, without being able to explain to him the true reason, plus the added stress of travelling with ten thousand pounds, in cash in my handbag. These were times that I was fully aware that I had no one in Switzerland to turn to. I was exhausted physically and mentally on my return.

At a certain point I realised I had to get help, so, I turned to Gary's company, they were in complete disbelief I think, and they offered the help of their Lawyer, I breathed a sigh of relief, fully confident that a Lawyer would be able to sort this matter out for me. The Lawyer advised me that the best option was to apply for a Kesb, in other words a Power of Attorney, I duly obtained the forms, filled them in and returned them, stating the reasons why I needed the Kesb and attaching a letter from the Doctor, along with the fee of Eight Hundred Francs, which I thought an outrageous amount for printing off a generic piece of paper with a stamp on, however, if this was the way forward then I had no choice. I sent a copy to the Lawyer and he checked it and confirmed I would get full control of all Gary's financial affairs.

The document was presented to the Bank manager, who told me it would be sent to head office that day, and they would then send papers for me to sign, and also new debit cards in both our names. All very simple now, or so I thought. I was now able to get my mind fully focused again on Gary and his therapies.

Four days passed by with no word from the bank, which did not amuse me one little bit, so I called and asked if there was any word, the Manager said yes and could I come in to the branch, an appointment for 08.00 hrs the next day was made.

I was slightly annoyed that I had had to instigate the contact but decided to let it go as things were nearly sorted. It was all very polite on my arrival, hand shaking and offer of coffee which I declined, and off to his office. The news that came next was almost too much for me to take at this point, head office had overturned the Power of Attorney.

I could not believe my ears, I just sat in silence and disbelief. After what was now almost four months and eight hundred Francs, not to mention flights to the UK and Spain and back, I was exactly where I started. I asked him how they could make this decision, when I had a Kesb, and exactly what did they expect me to do financially.

He informed me that any bills with Gary's name on, could be brought to the bank and paid. I asked him. "What about money for living expenses like petrol and food, I have to go to the clinic every-day?" He said that unless it was directly for Gary, then I could not submit a receipt. I just could not believe what I was hearing, I had to get out of that office, I could not look at him or speak further, so I took my coat and started to walk out, he tried to cajole me but I was not listening, I needed to call the Lawyer. I needed to calm myself first, before I reached the clinic and Gary.

All day at the clinic I could not get my mind away from the bank problem, I did not need this distraction, I just wanted to be there fully for Gary, and I had no idea what the Lawyer's reaction would be, so as soon as I had the chance I sent him an e mail, giving him an update.

I received a call from the Lawyer, he said he had no idea why the bank had acted the way they had, he had checked the Kesb and it said exactly what I needed it to. He said he would write to the bank and get back to me once he received a reply. I waited one week, getting more impatient each day for the Lawyer to contact me, no call was forthcoming, so I called him. As if it was nothing of importance, he said that apparently the bank has the right to overturn the Kesb. To say I was dumbstruck is a complete understatement. So I paid eight hundred francs for a useless piece of paper was one of my first thoughts, rapidly followed by what do I do now.

I asked the question of the Lawyer "what do we do now then?" He said to my complete horror, there isn't anything we can do really, the bank have made their decision. " But I am his wife" was my retort, the Lawyer actually chuckled on the other end of the phone and said, " Mrs Yates Swiss bank accounts are secure, no one gets into them without permission from the account holder, and as far as being his wife, it's the wives that most men are hiding their money from". He thought this was highly amusing. I replied, "Well obviously the Swiss do not have the same marriages as we do. So now where did this leave me? Right back at the beginning again.

My next steps were to ask the bank to send a letter to Gary, authorising me to take over his accounts and he would sign it, I was told it is too late now as you have Power of Attorney so he is not deemed competent enough to sign it. I offered to bring Gary to the bank and the Manager could ask him if he understood what he was doing, which of course he did, and was fully aware and happy for me to take control. This is not possible was the reply. After several visits and phone calls, I suddenly realised that I was getting nowhere, and further action on my part was necessary. The situation was desperate now and so was I.

The very next evening was spent on the internet, researching the rights of the bank customer. Very interesting, I found out that you can request a meeting with Head office, and they have to see you. Armed with my new information, I dropped into the bank unannounced the very next morning, asked for the Manager and was taken to his office, I was amused and happy to realise that by now, there was a dread in his eyes at having to deal with me, that's a good thing, it puts them on the back foot.

Very directly I said, "I need you to make an appointment for me at Head office, I would like to see the person who is making the decisions, as I would like to see the whites of his eyes when he explains why he thinks the bank have more rights over my husbands money than his wife does" I pointed out that by law I have the right to this appointment, and if I don't get an appointment in the next three days, then I will be instructing Gary's Company Lawyer to take the bank to court."

There was no response, just a look of shock really on his face and I had left before he could gather himself. I felt very ready now, to face the accuser almost, someone who didn't know either Gary or myself, didn't know our lives together, but didn't think I had the right to look after his financial affairs, I felt my strength had returned and I was ready to do battle.

One of those moments happened again, that second in life that can change things, the next evening when I returned to the apartment, I picked up the post from our post box, climbed the six flights of stairs feeling weary from the day, very ready to just relax with a glass of wine for the evening.

Quite a lot of post, as seems the norm these days, most of which there is generally a problem sorting, so I threw it down on the table, deciding to leave it until the next morning. After a bite to eat and a glass of wine I was feeling relaxed and decided to tackle the post. I noted a letter from the bank, I felt a note of surprise at how quickly they had reacted and wondered if it would contain my appointment. To my total surprise, they had reversed their decision, and if I went to the bank, there was a document to sign and the new debit cards would be ready for me to pick up. Nearly five months of obstruction from the bank, the intervention of a Lawyer, eight hundred Francs on a Kesb, and all it took was a threat to take them to court. Sometimes the little man wins when he stands up to the big guy.

It wasn't just a feeling of victory, it was also making them realise that they can't just make these types of decision over people lives, its destructive at times like this and part of their service should be to help people in difficult situations, not block every direction you turn in. during this 5 month period, I have joked to Gary that his bank account is mounting up very nicely whilst mine is depleting rapidly.

I had already decided that once I had control, I would open a joint account with Gary at another bank and would get the Company to redirect his salary away from this original one. For certain they were about to lose a good customer, they did not deserve our loyalty as they showed us none. On the contrary, they were as obstructive as it was possible to be.

One important thing to take from this, is that everyone should try to make sure, that they are aware of the laws in the country that they are living in, should anything like our situation occur, or in fact the death of a partner. Life is hard enough when something devastating happens to either of you, being faced with such difficult matters to sort out, just makes the whole experience more heart-breaking, not to mention stressful, to deal with.

I have since learnt, that here in Switzerland, there is a document that Swiss couples both sign, which gives automatic access to each others financial concerns. If we had friends here at the time, no doubt they would have been able to advise me of this and we could have had this in place. Most people find it difficult to discuss such matters, the same goes for making Wills, but everyone should think about how to best safeguard each other during these unexpected events. No one can be prepared enough for tragic events, but you can put things in place to ease the problems.

It's not being cold hearted to discuss such serious things, it is being sensible and in fact caring about each other, Gary would never have wanted me to have gone through this stress and would have been very upset if he had known at the time, he has the ultimate trust in me and would just want me to be able to deal with our lives the best way I know how.

CHAPTER FOUR

We are four weeks into our unexpected journey.
We have found sunshine behind the clouds.
Music over the silence.
Warmth in the cold.
We have received strength from our therapists.
And support from our friends.

I have made a decision, I have no commitments here in Switzerland, just time on my hands, if I didn't spend time at the clinic, then what would I do? My days would be long and difficult to fill. I have no intension of leaving Gary for any period of time to travel to Spain or UK, unless it becomes a matter of urgency to do so again, I feel that my presence at the clinic is both beneficial to Gary's recovery and also his mental state.

I have asked the Doctor if it would be alright to continue coming to the clinic every-day to support Gary, the answer was a resounding yes. So far it has proved to be a very positive decision, allowing me to learn about his therapies and then able to instigate them during his free time, and to keep Gary's mood as positive as is humanly possible in this situation. I do have to say, that Gary's overall mood is very upbeat and happy, but I also know that this is due partially to the anti - depressant medication, which after speaking with the doctor about it, I realise this is definitely necessary at this point. Neither Gary or myself, has ever been a believer in taking medication of this type, but then neither of us has suffered from depression, so I am by no means an authority on the subject.

I have to bring some of our personal life back, it is important for Gary to see that our life together is still intact, albeit very different. Music and dance were a large part of our lives, we love music and we love to Salsa dance.

Every morning now, when I arrive, and we are ready to sit, with a coffee in the corridor before therapy begins, I play music on my iPad, first I play the same two songs every day. Firstly, 'Somewhere Over The Rainbow', the Israel KamaKawiwo version, it's something I have done for a long time, and I call it my morning sunshine song, after that it's 'You

Are The Reason', by Callum Scott. This has become our song, the words are so poignant for me, I listen to it every day in the car.

This special time in the morning is how we come together again each day, it's how I show him that we are still the same people we always have been, still close in everything we are searching for in life. He is so lost in his mind, no one else features in his daily thoughts but me. He has already refused to have any visitors here, even his parents, which is very hard for them, they are of course desperate to come and see him, but I have to respect his wishes for now.

However, I accept that the longer he feels like this, the harder it will be for me to keep putting them off, but I will have to deal with this as I think fit. So, for now, I have to be his all, and that is acceptable for as long as he feels safe with this decision. He is not ready to face the outside World yet and I prefer to allow him to feel comfortable in this safe environment for the time being.

Our days are taking on a routine now, when he is not in a therapy class, we sit at our table and practice writing with his left hand, amazingly he seems to master it very quickly, his writing is very neat considering he is right handed, it is a great positive step for him. we start with the Alphabet, I write the letters and he can trace over them, soon he is able to copy below them. We spend time every-day, practicing whatever therapy he has been to, whether it is writing, memory games or the physical stuff like balance class.

We no longer need the auxiliary lady to take us to sessions, and we are made very free to roam around the clinic and to use the therapy rooms by ourselves.

During the therapy sessions, I generally sit at the back of the room where Gary can't see me, if he can, then he tends to look to me if he doesn't understand anything, I only join in if they need a translation or help with personal questions. It is of course, not the norm for a family member to be present every-day, most people have a visitor maybe one evening and at weekends, and I am aware, that some therapists are not as comfortable as others, but this is not a concern to me.

I am somewhat of a curiosity around the clinic, particularly as I stand out so much with my clothes, of course that's not hard as patients of course, mostly wear tracksuits and staff wear uniforms. As time goes on, we form kind of friendships with a few people here, mostly the staff, there are no other English patients that I have come across so far, which is another reason I feel a need to spend time with Gary, it would be so difficult for him to integrate with the other patients, not least that he has no speech, but also the language barrier. The thought of him being alone so much in his spare time, just fills me with heartache.

I have always felt very lucky and appreciate, that I was in a position to be able to walk away from my life in every aspect, and commit my time to Gary, I do understand of course, that not many people in this situation would have that possibility, or would be able to change their lives to such an extent or even contemplate it. This does not mean their decision is wrong, it just means that it is right for them. I am in the enviable position that I am not answerable to anyone, and no one relies on me, and of course I am financially stable. I just knew from the start that this was the right decision for Gary's future recovery. The World and everyone I know in it, will go on admirably without me for now. I hope that our friends and family will be there to welcome us back at the end of our journey.

The important thing for people is to be there when they can, and to offer quality time, to try to keep as much normality to life as is possible, and I mean the simple things in life. Our coffee breaks in the coffee shop everyday are a good example, it is time out from focusing on "The Stroke." In helping Gary's recovery, it entails focusing on all the things he cannot do, when we are not doing that, I try to focus him on the things he can still do, just like walking to the coffee shop, drinking coffee and chatting, interacting with the staff, even though we have limited language ability we can still manage to converse. Everyone here is used to working around stroke victims, we are not facing curious stares, or sympathetic glances, so Gary's problems fade into the background at leisure time.

It's important to remember that the person who has had the stroke, is longing to be better, they just want things to go back to how they were, they are missing every aspect of their life, so the more things you can think to do with them from that life, the better they will feel.

At this point, it is difficult to imagine how you can do things together that will remind him positively of those good times, and at the same time give hope , so I have thought hard about it, and made a list.

He can walk, albeit, slowly and unsteadily, but I will be by his side, to make sure he never falls, so walking is a good outdoor pursuit, and we have such amazing grounds here, built for therapy walking, such as different surfaces, gravel, stones, grass, uneven paths, that sort of thing, so we will walk around every day, no matter what the weather, it will help with his walking and also with his wellbeing. We will not get the lift; we will take the stairs so he will get stronger and more independent over time. Not everywhere we will go in the future will have a lift, not least our apartment, if he is ever going to be able to come home for the weekend in the near future, he has to be strong enough to take six flights of stairs. One of the best ideas so far, is dancing. I know Gary believed that our Salsa dancing days were over, and this would hurt him deeply, not least because he knows I love it, so I have our favourite Salsa dance record on my iPad, and that is "George Michael's, '*My baby just cares for me*' , from his Symphonica Album", it is one we have danced to endlessly at home in our Spanish kitchen after many a night out.

I have decided that every afternoon, in the corridor, we will dance to our record. That is provided Gary subscribes to the idea.

The first afternoon I play the song through for him, he looks at me with a very sad expression, so I say to him "can you walk?" He nods "yes". Then I say, "can you hold my hand"? he nods yes again, "well in that case I think we can still dance to our favourite record". If I could describe the look on his face I would, but I fear I do not have the words for that, so I will leave it to your imaginations.

I stand and take his hand, he is still very unsure whether or not I am being serious, I smile and say, "come on let's give it a go, you can do this." He has such faith in me and such trust, and this was proof of that fact, with the usual difficulty, he gets out of the chair, I start the music and off we go.

He does not remember the sequence but I lead him through it, he is very unbalanced but I hold on tight to him, he can't spin me around, but I let him feel he does, he doesn't do it like he did by any stretch of the imagination, but he gives it a good try, and his smile says it all. I tell him how great he is, and that if he can do what he is doing at this stage of his recovery, then we can only imagine what is to come. He looks so happy, genuinely happy, he gives me such a big hug and kisses me. Life just got normal and my husband is carefree for three whole minutes.

When we started to dance, most people tried to ignore us, pretending it wasn't happening, that's just the Swiss way, but a member of staff comes out of the office to see what the music is about, she calls the other staff who are inside, the staff are really interested and happy to see us, they look surprised at first but soon they are smiling.

After we finish our dance, they give us a little round of applause, and Gary claps for us also. This simple thing, that was so important to us before, is still important now, so I refuse to allow this stroke to take it away from us. Everything about this is good for Gary's physical recovery and mental well- being, and do I care what anyone thinks, no I don't, was Gary embarrassed, for about five seconds only, then dance, music and happiness flooded into his soul, and made him believe again.

I tell him that this is just the start, our journey will have many pleasures in it, many happy times to remember. Everyone's life is a journey, but not everyone takes the journey and makes it their own. We will mould this journey, we will travel it our way, and we will make just as many happy memories as we did before, we will not carry with us on any part of this journey, any sadness or failure. We will not become victims of something that could not be predicted, we will fill our hearts and souls with gratitude at having the chance to travel this adventure together, we will soar high on each -others enthusiasm and hope.

CHAPTER FIVE

Hope does not make the tears sting less.
Hope does not make the journey easier.
Hope does not make your heartache less.
Hope just leads us forward.
Without hope you will flounder.

It is so important to add hope to life, some people find it hard to hope for the best, I have often said during times in my life, when I didn't know how things were going to work out, "I expect the worse but hope for the best". This way I always had the feeling that things could be ok, but if things didn't turn out quite how I wanted them to, then I was kind of prepared for it. For me this seems to work at covering all bases, and now is no time to change my philosophy.

The only way you can heal from something like this, is to make your 'Now Life', the best it can possibly be.

Our 'Now Life' is all about Gary's recovery, but it is also about living the best life we can muster in this situation. We will accept that his home for now is the clinic and be grateful for the help he is getting. We will add things into life as and when we can, like music and dancing, like being the together couple that we have always been, I will not let him dwell on what has happened and the things he cannot do for now, but remind him of the things that we can still do and the things that he may still be able to do in the future. We don't know, and no one can tell us at this time, what his recovery will be or what he will eventually be able to achieve, so our focus is on what he achieves each day.

Gary's memory loss, is sometimes a blessing I think, he doesn't mourn the loss of our Spanish home for now as he doesn't remember it, but strangely he does remember his motorbike, so he is mourning that, he doesn't remember his children so he has no emotions about that, he recognises his parents, but doesn't remember their names as yet. I think he is sad when he thinks about them having to deal with this, and I think this could be one of the reasons that he doesn't want them to see him like this. I have asked him if there is anyone that he wants to see and he shakes his head, this confirms to me that his emotions are intact, and he has a proper understanding about what has happened. He is very proud and that is one of the reasons he does not want anyone to see him. His best friend Paul, immediately offered to come over to support us, but he very adamantly said no, I can understand how he feels, and I will always hope that these people will also understand why I couldn't allow them to come.

Gary is still his own person, and in this situation we must never treat them like children, they are still adults and they are still entitled to take some control of their lives, it is a big mistake for anyone in this position to assume the role of a parent again. We are not parents we are still wives. Yes, it would be so easy to take control when they seem helpless, it's always quicker and easier at first to help too much, the idea of recovery is for them to do as much as they possibly can. It's that thing called "Tough Love", and it is one of the hardest things to do, when you see someone struggling. But you have to assess things very swiftly, and take a step back, allow them to give it their best shot. I am no exception, sometimes I see him struggle with something and I have to turn away, pretend I am not aware of his struggle, I have to allow him to maybe find a different way of doing something, to compensate in some way. I have seen many times already, how he will manage to complete a task that I maybe thought he wouldn't. Independence is a priority gateway to achieving self-esteem and self- respect, no one wants to feel like a child again, it's just demoralising and destructive to any-one's recovery.

I talk to him about World news affairs, things that he would have been following every-day, the currency levels around the World, a particular part of his everyday work life, about politics around the world, you may think this is boring under our present situation, but he needs intellectual stimulation, he is a highly intelligent guy. I scan the daily paper to find things that he would have always found interesting. I go the extra mile and find out what is happening in the football world, Gary is a keen football fan, having been a very good footballer in his youth, playing at one stage for Aston Villa, I have no interest in football but these are the sacrifices one makes in the name of love!

He supports Liverpool so I have managed to find games on YouTube for him to watch on his iPad. This has several benefits, not least he can now put his passcode in, find 'YouTube' himself and find the last game played. Just a week ago he could not have done this. He now watches games when he is in bed and I leave for the night. This is good for both of us, I feel he will be distracted until he settles down for sleep and he loves watching it. I have also enlisted his father to send us details of when the matches are played, and this is a positive contact for his parents, they need to feel that they are contributing and are involved with what is going on in some small way. I am so aware that they have not been able to see Gary, that they just want some confirmation that he is ok, they have every day to just think about him, and every night to lay awake worrying about him, all they want to do is come to see him. I feel terrible for them but there is nothing I can do at this point and I can't have Gary stressing about it.

So, you see, a little thought about things can bring big changes to us all. It's all about remembering who that person is, what they like, what you can bring back to them, how you can adapt things to make them work still. It is very early days for us, but I am always thinking about this, and finding as many ways of bringing his life back to him. The happier he is every day, the better he will deal with his situation and the better I will feel. It certainly isn't about how much more comfortable I can make him in bed, or how much easier it is for me to feed him, or how much quicker it is if I button up his shirt, how much more convenient it would be for you to fetch the two coffees from the counter instead of him having to bring one and then go back for the other. It is about making him realise every-day that he is capable, it's just that simple, don't take every job onto yourself, but ask yourself would they be happy letting you do everything, I know my husband wouldn't be.

Sometimes, he will look to me to do something, if I think he can do it, then I just say "I think you can manage that" or "I'm not your butler", he knows exactly what I mean and he gets on with it, after all, as I often tell him, we have no rush, you can take as long as you like.

Sometimes when we are going to a therapy session on a different floor, he makes for the lift, I just look at him and head towards the stairs, I say "if you want to get the lift then it's your decision but I am taking the stairs", or I simply say "use it or lose it" this has become one of my favourite wake up calls for him. He soon follows me to the stairs, and he knows that every day he gets stronger and more capable, and that's his reward.

When he does not want to go for a walk, I say "but it's not all about you, and I want some fresh air and you don't want to come with me?", and so the manipulation and guilt trips go on every day, but of course he knows this and he always gives me a wry smile. And he knows that there is always a nice coffee at the end of it.

Our walking is something of a novelty to most people watching from the clinic, it's not just about a walk it's about everything to do with walking, finding steps to take, trying to walk a straight line, walking backwards, anything that challenges him to use his balance more. At present, he uses his hip and swings the right leg to move it forward, and one of the problems he has which is common with this stroke is, "Drop Foot", which means he cannot put his heel down when he walks, so that makes his hip compensate, it also increases the chances of him catching his toe and falling, so I am always by his side just in case. This is something we need to work on continuously, and walking is the best answer. Next week we will be given daily use of the Clinic Gym, and we will be able to use the bikes and the treadmill, plus other equipment, this will be a really positive addition to his week.

His programme of therapies is extensive now, filling a good part of his day, but allowing time to rest and also giving us some quality time. We have settled into our own therapy sessions together at our table in the corridor each day, and during his rest time I get to sort paperwork, telephone calls and organising things I need to do. I also use this time to post my status on Facebook to keep everyone updated, and also check for messages from friends, which is always inspiring and very positive for me.

Everyone here knows our schedule, and I am always offered a coffee and biscuit by the reception staff when I am alone. Sometimes one of the members of the nursing team will sit for a chat with me, or the lovely Rosa Marie from reception will stop for a catch-up. It is amazing how quickly I have adapted my life to this World, from what it was just a short while ago, it is unrecognisable, but I never have any doubt that this is the right decision for us.

Gary seems as settled with his surroundings as he could be at this time, and he has no mood swings, his medication seems to keep him in a good place mentally, and he is now sleeping well I am told, and for this I am very grateful. However, he still has problems at night with his incontinence but we have an appointment to see the Urologist, and they have assured us that things will be sorted out with this matter, so as always I have every confidence in what they tell us, and I am looking forward to Gary not having to deal with upset too much longer.

It is such a great thing, that whenever he needs to see anyone about anything, it is all within the clinic, no having to get him to Hospital or Doctors' appointments, this facility provides everything, even as I have recently found out, a department to help me with anything official to do with Gary, so an appointment has been made for me next week. This is a weight off my mind as I have so many questions I need answers to, not least, what happens about Gary's job? In the UK I would be able to find out this information easily with a phone call, but I had no idea where to start with this, and again it is partially to do with the language barrier.

CHAPTER SIX

Smiling is the best way to face any problem.
To crush every fear as it appears.
And to hide pain from him.
Smile amongst the hurt and you will cheat it.

We are now well into December and my thoughts have started to turn to Christmas. I have already broached the subject and have been told that wherever possible people are encouraged to go home for Christmas, just one night allowed. There is a skeleton staff on at the clinic, and of course there will be the necessary staff to look after Gary if he stays here.

Now the problem is he can't come home as he is not ready or strong enough to climb six flights of stairs, and even if he could by then, the thought of spending Christmas, just the two of us in the flat, with no Christmas tree or trimmings, no family or friends popping in for drinks, trying to make a Christmas lunch for two, is a non- starter, I know for sure it would make us both very unhappy and magnify what has happened to our lives. I absolutely do not want us to spend Christmas in a clinic that will be half empty and very quiet, with little Christmas cheer, this would be a disaster for Gary's emotional state. We love Christmas and always celebrate it to the full, this year needs to be the same as much as I can make it.

I need to see the doctor, to put my plan to her and see if she will agree to it, before I mention it to Gary.

I have made my mind up that I will not allow this to be remembered as the worse Christmas ever, it's all about limiting the impact this stroke has on life, so, I have decided that if I am allowed, I will drive us the three hours , over the border to St Anton in Austria, one of our favourite ski resorts, we go there every year for weekends and holidays. We have great memories of fun times there.

I already know that patients are allowed to stay overnight on Christmas eve, but must return by 19.00 hrs on Christmas night. This is very do-able without Gary getting too tired, and he can doze in the car if he needs to. It is a trip we have driven numerous times.

When I see the doctor and put my plan to her, she looks a little surprised to say the least, but I explain it all to her, and tell her my reasons, she happily agrees to the plan providing she feels that Gary's progress carries on, and she thinks it is a very exciting idea, she adds, that if she can't trust Gary with me then she can't trust him with anyone. My plan is in progress.

Gary is overjoyed when I tell him about our next adventure, I also tell him that this will be the best Christmas I can make it, and we will look back on it with good memories instead of sad ones. He is all for it, and I feel so happy for him, he now has something to look forward to over the next couple of weeks, and this is how life should still be, even after a severe stroke, don't just give in to settling for what is expected by others, or what you think is the sensible or only option, there are always options if you look for them.

I spend this evening at home, planning and booking. I am of course fully aware that it is almost impossible to book a room for one night during the Christmas period, and that it is very late to be expecting to book our favourite Hotel for one night, I explain to the owner, who knows us well, about Gary's stroke, prior warning gives them the opportunity of being prepared, and no embarrassing moments for any of us. She say's "of course, I will find a room for you".. She also books us a room on the ground floor, before the need to request one. I ask if she still has room for us to have Dinner on Christmas Eve and Christmas day lunch, she said she would make sure there was a table for us. She was very shocked to hear the news and assured me that they would do everything to make our stay special. it doesn't get more helpful than that, and I was very touched by her attitude. In this situation, people can either make it easy or difficult, and I am to become even more aware in the future, of how different businesses react to disability, and have an even greater understanding and empathy towards disabled people and the problems they face when travelling and staying away from home, than I did before this happened to Gary.

I make my mind up very quickly, that I would never allow anyone to make Gary feel like a second-class citizen, in any situation, and I would be quite prepared to stand up to anyone who tried. I have often said, generally, that the hospitality trade sometimes has the least hospitable staff ever. I have said on more than one occasion when I had received bad service, “It’s all in the title, Customer Care”, and “If you’re not happy in your work then get another job”

Next I make a booking for Christmas Eve lunch, as I expect to arrive mid- morning. My itinerary is in progress, and I love an itinerary. I am by nature a planner, all my friends know this and if we are going on a trip or meeting for dinner, anything at all, they always entrust the planning to me, I am that saying, “Give a job to a busy person and it will get done fast”.

So, my plans are in full swing, and the main organising is done, so we can chat about it over the weeks and look forward to Christmas as always. I will order Gary some presents online, so he has something to open on Christmas morning, the true benefits of the internet at a time like this. Priceless.

I am even considering treating myself to a new dress, I have nothing here really other than ski gear and very warm casual clothes, as I was never here in the Spring or Summer, I may have to order online as I doubt very much that I will be able to find anything to my taste here, but not only that, everything here, is super expensive, I still have time to address that, and it’s not a major concern if I do or I don’t, it would just be nice. Gary on the other hand has several suits and nice shirts, so he is sorted.

I feel a great sense of achievement, and excitement, Gary has a favourite music bar in St Anton, and we will go there, I think it will be so good for his spirit to be able to rise again, to join in with something we love, listen to the music, be part of the crowd.

I am very aware, that being around skiers, will bring its own sadness in part, but as I tell him, no one knows whether he will be able to ski again or not, and for now we have to be happy to be a small part of things, and hope that the future will bring skiing back into our lives.

CHAPTER SEVEN

There are frustrating days,
but never bad days
I remind him everything is possible,
if you believe in yourself.

Gary's therapies are very bitter -sweet at times, in these early days, we are finding out how much the Aphasia is affecting him, and how much damage the injury to his brain has caused. It is becoming very apparent, that Gary struggles to understand things, simple things, like "Put your arm up" for instance, basic things like "Put your shoes on". I have to do the action or show him the object, then he will understand. Another example is that he is told every-night, by the staff and by me, that if he needs the toilet or anything else at all, he must use the call button at the bedside, but every night, if he wants to get up for the toilet for instance, he forgets to call someone, instead the staff see him appear in the corridor. They are of course concerned that if he is not fully awake, he may stumble and fall. No matter how many times we tell him it does not register. His walking is not stable, and he struggles getting out of bed, but he still does it, this just shows his determination.

He has no idea what any object is, so I have decided to take four everyday objects and ask him, throughout the day, to pick each object out as I say them. So, whilst he is watching, I show him a pen then draw it, I write pen below it, I do the same with a pair of glasses, a key and a glove.

After I have drawn them, I ask him. "Which is the pen?" If I could describe to you fully, how Gary studies each object, it would be to say, it was with such an intensity it was unnerving. No matter how long he studies the four pictures he just cannot identify them and pick them out. Even though the word was written next to the object it made no difference. If I do the same with the actual objects it was the same outcome. I repeat this exercise every day, three or four times, but there seemed to be no improvement.

After one week of the recognition exercise, I decided to see if doing the action of the object would help. I said to him "which are the glasses? I then mimed putting on glasses, he immediately picked the glasses out! And the same with the other three objects. Now we were getting somewhere. Half an hour later I asked him again, and he didn't know, but if I mimed it again, he knew. I didn't know what this really meant, other than his short- term memory was that bad, but I felt it was a positive and I would tell the therapist later.

Very soon things got even more complex, I drew the objects again, this time I put the four words along the bottom of the page, first I asked him if he knew what the word Pen meant, he nodded yes, I asked him if he could point to the pen, he suddenly picked up a pencil from the table and drew a line from the word Pen to the drawing of the Pen. He could read associate. This shows just how complex the brain is, he can draw a line from word to object, but he can't point to it, if I just say the word. If I point to the word Pen and ask him to show me which one it is, he will trace his finger from the word to it the drawing of the object.

To realise that he has such difficulty recognising every-day objects is very disturbing, and the fact that he cannot differentiate between an elephant and a bed for instance, is pretty mind blowing.

I start to think about my lovely husband, this highly intelligent person who had such a successful career, and I think about all the fantastic knowledge he has, and how it is all still there, none of it has been lost, it is all just trapped in a maze, a maze that is preventing him from accessing it. His speech is still there, perfectly intact, but unable to make the journey down the speech channel. I think of it like this, he can see the word in his mind, he knows what it is and how to say it, but when it gets into the speech channel it gets trapped in a chicane, due to the injury, there is no direct route anymore for it to get through. It just gets trapped and nothing comes out. This is my way of seeing it, and trying to understand it, I am sure the medical World has a better way of explaining it, but this is my way for now.

I ask myself. "What is the way forward?" The speech therapist talks all the time about alternative methods of communication, drawing, writing key words, his phone, computer, word boards and these such things. But I have thought about this a lot, I know my husband very well, and this will not be a good solution moving forward. He has always been a chatter box, the life and soul of any gathering, he will want to join in with conversations and it will not work for him having to try to join in by writing things down. For him to integrate back into normal life he will need speech. Yes, it is a help for now, of course, but speech is a very integral part of his life and we need to make them understand this. I consider what they are doing here, and come to the conclusion, that here, everyone is treated the same, it is text- book learning, they have a method and use it on everyone.

Of course, I understand that everyone who comes here is just passing through for a period of time, and they need to give people tools to work with that they can use when they leave. So, I decide that we have to work alongside of them, we don't have to just work with their tools or at their pace, they are here to help guide us on this part of the journey. What I think is important is that we have our own map also, a map that will enable us to find short cuts on steep hills, we don't just have to go at the slowest pace, because that's what everyone else does. If we can find short cuts then we will take them, and our journey will progress faster.

There has to be a way of unlocking his speech as the injury starts to heal. If there is a way, we will find it. They say that the speech is the hardest and last thing to come back, we understand this, so we have to be patient, of course, but we also have to find the best methods for Gary, we have some of the best people around us, to help with this.

However, it never hurts to research things for yourself. If I have a greater understanding of problems, then like most people I can start to unravel things and find a solution, I have learnt already, that the best form of therapy is repetition, everything I read about stroke recovery mentions this, the more repetitions you do the faster the brain will learn again, and this is both mentally and physically. Take 30 children in a classroom, they will all work and learn at a different pace, but you wouldn't make a gifted child, for instance, work at the pace of the slowest child in the class, or try to make the slowest child keep up with the gifted child, of course not, this would not work for either. It is my desire to find the best pace for Gary, the pace that keeps his belief in his recovery, priority to his wellbeing.

Every-day at the therapy sessions, it's virtually the same format, whether it is speech training or balance class. What I do, is take what he does in each class and then try to adapt it more to every-day life. For instance, he is trying to get some grip back in his hand, so when we go for coffee, I put his right hand around the glass then he closes his left hand around it, he then drinks like that, although the injured hand is not actually holding the cup, it is doing the action supported by the other hand. The hope is that the brain will eventually recognise the action of the right hand.

Another example is with speech, every-time I ask Gary something now and he nods his head, I say "Yes" and now he can repeat it, the same with "No", he still can't say it spontaneously himself, and other words he just can't form, but it is a great start.

The speech loss is the hardest to understand, as previously said, Gary has not lost his voice, he has just lost the channel to get the words out. But here is a strange thing, and this happens to most stroke sufferers, most will have a word, I think of it as a key word for them, now Gary's word has suddenly arrived, and it is "Cheers". At first it made me laugh, but after a short time, I realised it was a great word for him, he can use it very often. When someone say's 'Hello' to him, he says cheers, when they say 'Goodbye', he says cheers. If he wants to say thank you, then "Cheers" is just perfect. So very quickly, Gary found some control over his speech, and although it is a very small word, it gives him some much needed power.

It's not always this easy of course, some people's key word is not always appropriate or helpful. Some people do not have such socially acceptable words, a little on the Turrets scale, which can be upsetting for members of their family, and others have indistinguishable words, that don't appear to mean anything, and they can often repeat the word, Cheers was always a common word in Gary's vocabulary, and one that most people can associate with in any situation. Most importantly, it is a communicating word that he can use all the time.

I start to wonder if a person's key word has anything to do with their personality. Does it make a difference what type of background you come from? Or what your education status is? Is it gender aware? Does it make a difference how old you are? I will make a point of asking these questions, interesting, I think.

Here is the next amazing breakthrough with his speech. We have been going through the alphabet, saying the letter and seeing if any word for each letter comes to him, we did this starting with A and going through to Z , I would say the letter but also have it written down for him to see, if he couldn't form anything then I would say the simple answer, A- Apple. We did this for maybe four days, twice a day, but there was nothing so far, then suddenly I said L and he came straight out with "Love you", what a surprise and a beautiful one too. It took me so by surprise it did make my eyes water.

"I love you" was to become one of Gary's key phrases, and still is to this day. Whenever he sees friends or family, he will tell them, "I love you", it melts every-one's heart, and often, people say it to him before he has a chance to say it first.

I spoke to the Doctor about it and asked her the question, "does it make a difference what type of personality you are, where your key words or phrases are concerned?" She told me that it could, for instance if you were the type of person who used bad language commonly in every-day speech, then you were highly lightly to use it commonly after a stroke, she also said that my Husband must have a kind heart, as his words are always nice ones, and I agreed with her, he has one of the softest hearts of any man I know. But he uses it wisely, he does not waste his emotions on people who don't deserve them.

I have also heard that, if you speak a second language before a stroke, then it is very possible you will just revert back to your first language and not remember the second one at all.

As I spend every-day with Gary, we obviously converse all the time, so I try to make sure he has a method of answering or asking for things. One method that works very well, are hints, for instance, if I ask him what he wants to drink and he wants coffee, he puts his thumb under his chin and presses, then this means the word starts with a "K" sound, when he does it he will now say Coffee, if he puts his forefinger on his throat, that means the word is a "G" sound, so if I ask him "What is your name? ", He will touch his throat and will say Gary. If he puts his forefinger at the side of his mouth, it is a "P" sound, and he knows it means Pauline.

One time when I asked him "What do you want to drink?" and was expecting him to say coffee, he put his thumb under his chin and said "Cappuccino", this caused laughter with the staff and a round of applause, so it is a progressive way of getting him to use words in the correct way. Our form of sign language, and a way forward for now.

The Stroke

Something I have noticed, is that when Gary does talk, his words form correctly, and he has intonation. I have had contact in my past, with many people who have suffered strokes, some not so severe, and they have suffered speech loss the same, but once the speech starts to return, the words are not clear, often they appear to be slurring, almost like when some people have had too much to drink, the sentences are also very flat, no intonation, or expression. So, I often remind Gary of this as a positive for him.

Although Gary's vocabulary consists of very few words, he will use spontaneous words or even sentences, but they are not locked into his speech, they just happen in a situation. For example, I was talking about needing to get some food as I haven't anything much at the flat, he suddenly just said " you need to go shopping", the first time it happened I felt overjoyed, I thought to myself, " it's suddenly coming back, he can form a sentence ", I was so happy and relieved. But I was soon to have that bubble burst, it does not mean that he will ever say that sentence again any day soon. Spontaneous speech is common, but does not mean the speech is actually recovering suddenly, but it was something good for Gary to hang on to, and it shows that he can get sentences down the speech channel, and that despite the brain injury he can still form sentences to fit the situation, so that has to be a very good positive for us.

He is so patient, he will allow himself to be guided, he climbs each and every step with courage and strength from within, he trusts my strength to hold him and not to let him slip.

His faith in life is not so strong these days, we never believed in 'Blind Faith' before, we never do anything blindly, his trust is in me, my steady hand leads him safely through every step of the journey.

Gary has no past and does not know what the future holds, he lives in the here and now, each minute in time is all he thinks about, the things he doesn't remember, can't bother him, it's the things he knows he has lost that upset him, so we steer clear of any type of upsetting recall, we live today. Time has no relevance to him, but that is just the same for me, it is standing still, here in this place for now, we are in a bubble of our own, and we will not be leaving it, I don't think, any time soon.

Normal life is going on all around me, nothing is normal in our lives, but I feel ok with that, I have put life on hold for now, I am at peace with it, it's just a moment in time, it will pass like time does, then we will just look back on it, and like all memories after the passage of time, some will be happy, some will fill us with laughter, some may bring a few tears, but what is for sure, there are moments that we will never forget for their "Beauty and Hope:.

CHAPTER EIGHT

Watching Gary working so hard,
to achieve his goals.
Is nothing but inspiring.
Seeing him reach them,
is amazing

It seems that the time has come that we can be trusted to leave the clinic for a drive out and a coffee for an hour, this is a testament mainly to Gary's immune system getting stronger. I have thought about where the best place would be to take him and I am not keen, to go to our village coffee shop, I think it is too soon, I can't explain why, it's just a feeling. To go into town would be too much walking for him, so I decided to ask him, and his reply, brought a wave of emotion to me. As I have previously documented, we both have motorcycles and biking has been a fantastic part of our lives, it is causing Gary so much heartache that I try to stay away from the subject, so it was with some surprise to me, when, after a struggle to understand his choice, that I realised he wanted to go to our favourite Biker coffee shop. When we are in Switzerland under normal circumstances, we visit this venue maybe once a week at the weekend, enjoying looking at the bikes, and all the bike gear, having a chat with the owner, who is a delightful lady called Claudia, she speaks excellent English, and she is used to seeing us in the showroom or coffee shop. My instant thought is, "What will her reaction be to Gary?" then my thoughts turned to Gary, I am sure this exercise will make us both sad. I voice my opinion to Gary, suggesting that maybe it is too soon to go there, but he is adamant he wants to go.

Saturday morning, and I am at the clinic as always, for 09.00, Gary is waiting in reception, I walked past him at first, not expecting him to be there, the receptionist, with a beaming smile on her face pointed to him. Instead of his usual T/shirt and joggers, he was wearing a shirt and jeans, and just looked like my lovely husband always did at the weekend. He was smiling broadly and looked so happy, my heart melted, and my soul soared so high I felt I would rise off the floor.

These and many other occasions in the future, will become times when I realise, how much has been taken from our lives. Just those small inconsequential, things like going out for a coffee, things we all take for granted, well they suddenly become big and special, things that were normal, every-day activities, suddenly, feel like magical excursions, this is why this book is entitled "Our Extraordinary Journey", because every day really is extraordinary, it's an adventure because we don't know when or what the end will bring.

I tell him he looks lovely, he says "I Love You", I feel like my heart will burst. He then makes me understand that he did the buttons up on his shirt himself, one handed, and he is so pleased with himself, my heart is truly bursting now, I am so full of admiration for this man of mine.

The drive to the Coffee shop is lovely, the scenery here is breath-taking no matter which direction you turn. This Country has it all. Snow-capped mountains, crystal clear blue lakes, rolling hills in a myriad of greens. There are streams flowing down from the mountains, the water cascading over waterfalls formed by rocks, with pine forests stretching as far as the eye can see.

Gary is very quiet, but not in a bad way, I can sense that he is soaking everything in, like he is seeing it for the first time. I realise that it is practically the same for me, I am seeing this World in all its beauty, I see it better than I did before, I have driven this route many times, but I wasn't looking before, now I am acutely aware that we are travelling this route together on a different level, I understand again, how lucky we are to be doing this adventurous journey together. I ask him, "are you ok?" He answers with a nod and a smile, I say, "it's beautiful, but it would not be so beautiful if I was making this journey alone, do you see how lucky I am today?" He thinks about it, then slowly nods his head and wipes a little tear away, of course he understands.

The Coffee shop, adjoins the bike showroom, I hold onto Gary's arm as we walk across the Car Park, I can see Claudia inside, so I avert my eyes and start making for the Coffee shop, I am nervous all of a sudden, not for myself but for Claudia really, of course she will be shocked and I don't want to upset her. But Gary has other ideas, and is making for the Showroom, I asked him "do you want to go into the Showroom?" he nods,

I take a deep breath, and feeling a little light- headed, allow him to guide us forward.

I see she is looking very confused, not certain whether she should come over to us, or not, so I take the lead and call "Hi" to her, she heads towards us, at this point Gary takes himself slowly over to a bike. I know he wants me to explain things without him listening. I quickly explain what has happened, she understands and takes back her control, going to Gary and acting as she always does, very warm and friendly.

I realise that since this adventure began, this is the first time we have ventured out into the "Normal World", I also realise that to integrate back into a normal life, we will have to face many times of uncertainty, possibly many times of dealing with people who don't make the transition so calmly, not because they don't want to, but merely because they are closer to us and more emotional towards us.

From this experience, I realise the quicker I can get everyone to move on from their first reaction, is absolutely the best. I have taken this little bit of knowledge, I will use it, and I thank Claudia, who through her calm acceptance, has taught me something, and helped us along our journey.

We take a table in the window and order coffee, bikers come and go, it would be impossible to describe my feelings completely, I am happy we are here, at the same time it is completely screwing me up inside. Seeing all the lovely bikes, all I can think about is my bike, locked away, Gary's bike locked away, probably never to be ridden by us again. I think about how I will feel having to sell them. I watch Gary for a minute from the corner of my eye, he looks wistful, I wouldn't describe it as sad, more dream- like, as though he is in a different place in his head, then I realise he is. I want to tell him it is all going to be ok, I want to tell him not to be sad, but I just let him enjoy his own moment, as I know it will only be brief, and bitter- sweet.

I have been on many difficult journeys in my life, but I rank this as not just the hardest, but I fear that it will be the longest, this journey is not just about me, I have to manage it for the both of us. If I don't manage it well, then I will not be the only sufferer, I have to make this journey work to the very best of my ability. At the end of the journey there has to be a wonderful view that will compensate for everything.

The Stroke

CHAPTER NINE

It's not what happens to you in life,
that creates the path you follow.
It is what you do with it,
that shapes your journey.
Our Journey may have changed,
but we will not allow it to change our life together.

As well as the mental problems, Gary's physical problems are multiple, so we don't have the luxury of concentrating on one thing at a time, there is a window of time that we can work with, where the best recovery is possible, so we have to work everything, to its fullest at the same time. But it is also a fact, that for the brain injury to heal, it needs rest. The injury heals whilst it is sleeping. After a stroke, a person can crave sleep, sometimes when they don't even need it. Getting the correct amount of rest is very important, but life has to have structure and meaning.

I feel that it is my job to keep the meaning in our lives intact, to stop Gary from thinking that his life, our life is over, it would be so easy to sink into self- pity, wallow in the, "why me?" It should not come down to asking yourself, " why me?" if anything at least ask yourself, "why us?" This didn't happen to me, it happened to Gary, but I am an integral part of his life, and everything has always been about us, this is no exception. But there is no answer to "why us?", and asking the question is a waste of time and emotions. It can happen to anyone at any-time.

Just because you lead a healthy lifestyle, don't smoke, drink moderately' have a good diet, does not mean you can't have a stroke, in the same vein, because you drink ten pints of beer at the weekend, smoke two hundred cigarettes a week, are overweight and unfit, does not mean you will have a stroke.

Generally, for me to accept things in life I need answers, this is no exception. Every specialist consultant will tell a stroke survivor, that smoking can be a contributory factor, although Gary was not a smoker, he was reminded of this many times, however, we sit and watch a high percentage of the nursing staff and many of the very same consultants, standing outside the clinic smoking, one particular consultant can chain smoke three cigarettes in a fifteen minute break. I find this irritating at best and completely angers me at worst. I cannot understand how, any consultant can smoke a cigarette at break, then face a stroke survivor and tell them not to smoke, and stink of cigarette smoke whilst doing it. One could imagine that they themselves don't believe it's that much of a hazard.

I have mentioned to several people about my observations, but they just shrug and say, "I know". For all the research into this field, no one can answer this question. The same as they don't know why a seemingly perfectly healthy person has a stroke in the first place. This subject will be a constant source of frustration to me. There are a much higher number of non-smoking stroke patients at this clinic than there are smokers, so in my view. statistically, you are more likely to have a stroke as a non-smoker. Maybe being in this atmosphere, is making me dissect things more, but for sure, the more I think about it the less answers I find, and the more absurd it becomes. Of course, these are only my thoughts, and my head is full of questions, I am only human, and it is of course frustration that makes me question things that I cannot control. But I remind myself constantly, of the saying, "Accept the things you cannot change and change the things you can".

Never accepting that something can't be changed, will just result in never accepting that life will move on and things can still get better. I know that we will come across many wide rivers that we feel we can't cross, but I know we will find another way around. We will face challenges that we can't over-come, and we will have to accept this, but we will find a compromise that will allow us to proceed with our journey. What we will never do, is accept that there is no way around the obstacle, to do this would be like taking a backseat on life as we know it, it's about coming up with an alternative route, a route that we can both manage together, a route that will still take us to the glorious view at the top of our mountain.

I am sure, that at this point Gary has nothing but doubts about almost everything, not least the tough journey he is embarking on, he will even doubt himself and his ability and strength to carry on, his focus will be hazy and make it difficult for him to see that the journeys end is possible, and with vision, achievable.

I have to show him that he will get stronger with every new step he takes, I have to convince him that I am strong enough for both of us for now, he needs to be sure that I am with him every moment. I will never allow those insecurities to creep into his mind, never allow him to think I will abandon him. We are in this together, it's just that simple.

I know it is difficult for some people to deal with a partner being sick, and especially long term- illness, everyone is different, and marriages are different of course. I asked a patient that we have become friendly with, "How often does your husband come to visit you? She replied, "He used to come twice a week, but he is bored with me now, he doesn't come to visit anymore, just sends me a text now and again".

I felt so sad for this lady, he is treating it as though it were her fault. Everything I feel when I think about this happening to Gary, is always that this was not his fault. Everything that has changed about our lives, is not his fault. It is very important for him, that I remind him of this fact, I will not allow him to blame himself. I will not allow him to feel sorry for me, I don't want anyone to feel sorry for me, I need positive people to interact with me.

Being around negative people is soul destroying for anyone, when we are in difficult situations, we need to feel as though our friends treat us as the same person we have always been. I am still capable of laughing and enjoying hearing about their lives, people should not be afraid to tell me that they had a good night out, or that they are going on holiday. Too many people, think because you are in a difficult place in life at the moment, that they should not talk about the nice things they are doing, this is not good.

Let me explain, I have been in contact with a good friend during these weeks, we chatted, and I asked her how things were, and what she was up to, nothing special to report was the reply. Recently, another mutual friend, mentioned in passing, that the other friend was on her cruise. I was surprised that she had not mentioned it to me. I sent her a message, saying I didn't realise she was cruising, and wishing her a great holiday, and maybe we would join her next year. She replied, saying she didn't like to mention it, as she felt bad about it for me!

The Stroke

Friends must realise, that because our life is a little on hold for now, that we don't expect theirs to be. Just because we can't go away, does not mean that we won't be happy that they are able to enjoy a holiday. We are more aware now than ever, that no-one should put things off, if you want to do something, do it as soon as you can, I have always believed in this, and if I complete my "Bucket List" in good time, I have the bonus of doing some of it all over again. I appreciate my friends, involving me in their plans, I am happy that they are enjoying life, please don't anyone feel bad about life going on, whether we are part of it or not, the World will still go around.

Summing up, friends should always remember, who I am, I haven't changed because of Gary's stroke, I still enjoy all the same things I did before, and I appreciate those girly chats just the same, I can still laugh and joke and I can still enjoy a gossip, this does not make me feel like a bad person, and Gary would be happy to know this.

CHAPTER TEN

The secret of being happy,
is accepting where you are now.
Making the most of everyday,
making the most of living.

The Festive Season is approaching, and it will not be passing us by, that's for certain. We have had the Clinic December Festive itinerary.

There is to be a Carol Service on Friday, in the Hall here, how lovely I immediately think. I show it to Gary and his reaction is not very positive, I say to him, "it will be nice," we will go. I get a very negative response, so yet again I have to use the blackmail card, but as always it works, and we are going. It is very difficult of course, when it comes to a social event, in this situation, I completely understand how hard it is for him to motivate himself, but that's part of my job now. He might feel it's difficult and he has every right to feel that, but I always explain, that everyone within this safe haven, is a survivor like him or family members, everyone is in the same boat, all struggling against the same tidal wave of emotions.

They have a Xmas dinner planned on another evening, which we will also be attending, and we will treat it, as much as we can, like any social event we would be going to.

I have one little black dress here, the one I would normally wear to the Company Xmas get together, which of course we will not be attending this year. Do I think it is appropriate for this Clinic dinner? Not really, but I have to give Gary a sense of who we still are, and we are those people who like to dress up to go out, so I will wear the dress and high heels, and bring him a nice outfit to wear.

I have never been the type of person to succumb to peoples opinion of how I dress, and this is no exception. As much as possible, I want Gary to feel normality coming back into our lives. For us to attend a Festive Dinner, wearing jeans and T/shirt, no matter where it is, would not give him the same perspective of the evening. It is very important that I can keep moving him forward, by taking his mind away from the daily

"Therapy Mentality". Ways in which I can divert his thoughts to include happy life, positive life, and even altering his expectations daily, and for the future ahead, this is my quest.

Our dancing in the corridor every afternoon, is an example of bringing his thoughts around to our life beyond the clinic, it has become something he really looks forward to, and everyone is used to seeing us and seems to enjoy the spectacle, it is proving good for both his confidence and for his balance recovery.

I watch him at balance class, and take some of the exercises they do, and adapt them into our dancing, adding moves like walking backwards for instance, of course I hold on to him, but with the music it seems to relax him more, getting him to turn around, a difficult move for him, but again, it seems easier when he is relaxed and does not have too much time to think about it.

Balance class is one of my favourite therapies to watch, often there is music, the atmosphere is very much that of a group having fun, but when you get stroke survivors with balance problems, doing balancing tasks, it's very amusing, to everyone involved, I likened it to watching six people staggering home after a very drunken night out, it made everyone laugh, and now it became even more fun. If people feel embarrassed or self- conscious about performing tasks in public, they are less likely to do them to the best of their ability, I know this to be true for Gary, once I made it funny, he became much more prepared to get involved, he visibly relaxed and enjoyed himself.

During balance class in the Gym, I have the time to sit and watch, and I can see from afar, what his weaknesses and strengths are, it gives me the opportunity to explore ways of integrating balance therapy into every-day activities.

In the Gym there is Table Tennis, we have watched people play, so one evening after dinner, I suggested we had a game, Gary could use his left hand. I have never been any good at any ball sport and I said to him. "You will still beat me left- handed" this brought a knowing smile to his face.

We played for a while, and as predicted, he was the better player, and due to his tricky balance, I had to chase the balls and pick them up, so great exercise for me.

After the tennis, we went for a coffee and during this quiet time, I thought about the tennis, and how well he played, great for his side- step balance and eye coordination.

So, I was thinking, how would he manage if I taped the bat to his right arm, he has no grip, but he has limited movement in the arm. I suggest it to him, and he is all for it. My thinking is, that he will be able to move the arm to reach the ball, this will be good for getting the brain to accept the arm back more.

Gary is very keen to give it a go, so I ask one of the nurses if I can have bandage and tape, which she duly gives to me. Off we go.

I tape the hand to the bat, comfortably, and to my delight, he can hit the ball back to me, he can also serve, it's not as good as with his left arm but that gives me a little more advantage. Joking apart, it is a brilliant move, I can only imagine of course, how good it feels for Gary to see his arm working, what a breakthrough for us. This is exactly what I mean about thinking outside the box, adapting situations to meet the criteria Gary needs to allow him to do these things. He is very happy, and so am I.

It's another accomplishment for the man who never gives in to adversity, he is open to challenge, and change to get better, to be back in control of his life.

CHAPTER ELEVEN

Define the word "Amazing"
Adjective:
Causing great surprise or wonder, astounding.

After a stroke, it is all about coping with everyday life, being able to deal with the normal activities, even simple things become difficult, some seemingly impossible. Finding a new route back is paramount. No one wants to become totally reliant on someone else for simple tasks, particularly losing their independence with their personal hygiene is very distressing. The faster anyone can take back control the better life will become again.

When someone has lost the use of an arm, and is very unsteady, they become frightened of using the shower or bath, I know Gary was very nervous in the beginning, and it is difficult for him to complete, what would be simple two handed jobs, like squeezing shower gel onto themselves, so alternatives have to be found. Sponges impregnated with soap are the perfect answer at first, but now he just has a body sponge and can easily apply shower gel to it. Taking lids off can be difficult, but it just takes a little bit of thought, not screwing the lids on things like toothpaste, aftershave, and anything else he needs, just resting the lid on top, is the simple answer. Completing his own morning rituals of showering himself and shaving himself, gave him back his privacy and he can create his own routine, but I have to understand that it takes longer, so I always allow plenty of time.

At first, I used to tie his shoe- laces, doesn't sound much, but another task he could not perform himself, I knew that he felt he was being a nuisance asking me, and truthfully, sometimes I used to imagine doing this long term, and have smiled to myself, thinking how would I manage to get down there and back up when I am old! But this was another easily sorted problem.

There is a way to fix the laces that make it easy for him, these things are not usually thought of as important by professionals, therefore they are not addressed, so it is about taking the time to think it through, then finding a method. I believe that there are alternative ways of doing almost anything, and I take every problem and find the way.

In this situation, when a partner suddenly relies on you, like they have never had to rely on you before, it may seem that it is not fair on you, but I have thought deeply about this, and I look back at all the times that Gary has supported me, in many different ways over the years, without question, he has done it because he loves me and always wanted to be there for me. The same is happening now for him, he needs my unquestioning support, and that is exactly what I will give.

It is for sure, a time that my wants and needs have to take a back seat, I accept this, and I am at peace with it, I tell him often that I am happy where I am for now, and he does not have to worry about me. I know he understands how my life has been turned upside down, but he does not need to think of it as me making sacrifices. He has to know and believe that I am doing this because he is the most important thing in my life. I reassure him of this every day in many ways. Again, at the risk of repeating myself, I never want him to feel for one second that this is his fault, I am fiercely protective of his inner calm.

For Gary to feel inner peace, will help to make him heal quicker, I arrive every-day at the clinic, with a nice outfit on, my hair done and make-up on, this way he knows I have made time for myself, and he sees the person he knows. If I was to arrive looking like I don't care, or that I am not looking after myself, it would upset him, his inner calm would be affected, this in its own way would affect his mood and his ability to concentrate on himself.

I talk to him about the contact and support I receive from Facebook friends, every day, I read their messages to him. He needs to know that I am not living in a solitary world when I leave the clinic, he is very aware that I have no support system here, so I have to reassure him that I am ok with this, and that I have contact with friends and family every day.

Facebook is what it is, but at a time like this, it is amazing how important it has become, people have changed towards us, and I have realised, good or bad, that there are friends and there are friends. During this time, some people I would have considered before to be good friends, have now been demoted to acquaintances, and people who were acquaintances have been promoted to good friends. I have become so aware now, that we can all become 'Out of sight, out of mind'. I have had to deal with those thoughts, but I have moved on from wasting my time, feeling upset because I don't hear from some people. I accept that people are busy, and some can let you drift away easily. Others, who you least expect to enter so deeply into your life at a time like this, surprise you to the point of feeling joy and it makes up somewhat for others. One thing is for sure, I will not blame or judge people, I will just recategorize them in our lives.

One set of people, who have been very supportive to us, are my ex clients, although I had to drop them, like the proverbial hot brick, many of them have followed our journey and support us with messages on a daily basis, I can truthfully say, that this comes as no surprise to me. Most of my clients have been loyal to me for many years, supporting me through various changes in my business, so them joining us in their own way on our journey is just a joy for me, and I will never be able to thank them enough.

Although we have only had our house in Spain for four years, we have many friends there, and the same can be said for many of these people, some were merely people we saw in the café bars and exchanged pleasantries with, some were more social, but most have been accelerated to a place within my heart, not least for their concern for Gary, but for their concern for my well-being, their interaction with me from afar, lifts my spirits every day,

I now know, that I can accept many people into my life, that previously I would have kept at arms
length, maybe because I felt that I didn't need more friends, or I just didn't see them for the nice people they were, sometimes I am guilty of being a social butterfly, but not actually letting people into my life fully. In times of difficulty, it's good to have a crowd around you to offer the hand of friendship. Each of those hands, is helping me on this journey and I am very humbled by them.

CHAPTER TWELVE

Normal every-day life goes on all around us,
we just skipped out for a while.
We need to find a new path for our journey,
one that will take us to a spectacular view.

Gary has settled in well now, his anti-depressant medication has kicked in and he always has a smile on his face, some days I think it could be a good idea for me to have one, I am joking of course. He is sleeping well, but is still on his sleeping tablets, and he seems peaceful in himself. I am fully aware that the tablets are the main support for his emotional coping mechanism, but that's ok for now, it's normal for everyone after a stroke, and he needs to be able to keep the nightmares out of his head.

I know that Gary has never been a person who believed in taking medication, and at some point, he will want to resist, we will assess and address this, as it arises, for now, he needs this help to boost his emotional state.

The day has arrived for the Carol service, after dinner, we go to his room and get ready, it is so nice to see Gary in normal clothes again, nice shirt and trousers and I have a nice dress on. He seems very relaxed and looking forward to it, a complete change from a few days ago, this is the help of the medication, but also, I have chatted to him about it, just to reiterate that it will be great for us, and no pressure on him. He has nothing to be nervous about, but of course that is easy for me to say, however, he seems quite relaxed about it, and I feel, he has gotten used to the idea now.

The Hall is beautifully decorated, a huge, floor to ceiling Christmas tree, sparkling with a thousand lights and silver baubles, an instant festive feeling to it, lots of people milling around, soft drinks being proffered to everyone as they arrive. The tree looks so wonderful, so I ask Gary if we can have our photograph taken in front of it, he agrees, we ask someone to take it. All of a sudden, a feeling of normality seems to flood into my heart, Gary is looking all around, he has a smile on his face, he puts his thumb up to other patients and staff members, and says "Cheers",

I have that confident feeling, that against all the odds, Christmas will be good for us, and that my plan will go ahead. This will be a Christmas to remember, and for happy reasons not sad.

The Hall fills up, we take a seat and there are song sheets for us, the atmosphere is not one of a rehab clinic, not one bit, it is filled with joy and chatter, people smiling and enjoying the festive feel of the evening, as school children start to file onto the stage, at the front there is a pianist seated at a beautiful shiny, black Grand Piano.

The Director of the clinic gives what I assume is a welcoming talk, as it is in Swiss, I can only translate a little of it. I hold Gary's hand and squeeze it, he looks at me and gives me one of his big but slightly lopsided smiles, lopsided due to his slight paralysis, still evident, but for me it just makes him look cuter. Simply, he looks happy, he looks relaxed and more like his old self, I am very moved that this small event has brought him back to me a little more.

As the piano starts to play, I look to my song sheet, and joke to Gary how I love Carols but am always sad that I am tone deaf, the choir starts first, and to my great surprise Gary starts to sing, he sings the whole Carol, I am so flabbergasted, I just sit staring at him, not a word coming out of my mouth. He can sing, I almost can't believe my ears, and he keeps looking at me and smiling like he can't believe it either. What a joyous moment for us. His brain injury has not affected the area where singing comes from. I could cry with joy.

The children sing Carols and the whole evening is a great success, so many nurses and therapists compliment us on how nice we look, and that gives us a great boost, who doesn't like a compliment? This has served to prove, that it is very important to enter back into real life as soon as possible.

This is our first festive social event; next we have the Christmas dinner to look forward to at the weekend. I have a very good feeling that Gary will now be looking forward to it, and his insecurities will for now recede.

This is great preparation for our trip to St Anton at Christmas, I am now, really getting excited about it, and will enthuse Gary with some of my enthusiasm. Life needs to be full, as much as is possible in this situation, with plans for nice trips and inspiring events, happy situations to look forward to. I will let him feel that life goes on just as spectacularly as we want it to. We have made a great start and there will be no stopping us now, I will focus him on the positives every day, and I will kick the negatives into touch. Sitting on a chair looking out of a window will not be the way forward for him.

We make our way back to his room, he has normally been ready for bed by 18.00 every night at the latest, it is already 19.30 and I expect him to want to retire to bed, so I am pleasantly surprised when he intimates that he would like a cup of tea. I ask the nurse if it's possible, and of course she is happy to oblige. We sit together at our table in the corridor for another hour.

Our conversation turns to our Christmas adventure to St Anton, I ask him if he has any worries or concerns about it, he shakes his head and puts his thumb up. I tell him that we are just the same two people that we always were, and together we are a great force, together we can achieve most things, and we have the rest of our lives to enjoy. He is happy tonight.

Once I have settled him in bed, it's time for me to wend my way home. It is snowing, so a steady drive is called for as it is such a winding road, but I am quite happy, there is no rush to get to the flat.

The scenery tonight on my drive home is like something out of a film, the trees are loaded with snow and they all look like perfect, pure white sculptures, each one unique, glistening reflections in the many ponds they stand around, the stars are gleaming so bright against the dark velvety sky, its truly breath-taking in every sense of the word.

As I pass by the houses, many have Christmas trees outside, decorated with a thousand twinkling lights, and some with decorative reindeers pulling sleighs. I am suddenly reminded how different this year will be, no excitement for trimming the house, or decorating a tree for every room. No presents beautifully wrapped to place under the tree. I have no enthusiasm for buying a tree for a flat that only I see. I just could not motivate myself to bother. There will be no presents from friends and family, we are too far away. I have ordered a few small gifts for Gary online, to open Christmas morning, I need to make it as happy as I possibly can for us both. The pleasure this year is not receiving gifts, I have no need for anything, the important part for me, is the giving of gifts to Gary. I hope it will bring Christmas cheer to him.

Christmas is at the forefront of my mind now, and I am trying to plan it perfectly, it will not be easy I know that, I have to consider everything. It will be cold, and I need to make sure he is warm, he walks very slowly and unbalanced, so I am aware that we need to be very careful in the snow. I have to make sure I take everything he needs with us, not least his medication, he is administered this by the nurses daily, I will have to take this over, he is on fifteen tablets a day, and some have to be taken twelve hours apart, so I will set alarms on my phone.

It is easy for me to carry on, planning and looking forward to our trip, but I often wonder how Gary feels, what is going around in his head. I discuss things often, always confirming that he is happy to do this trip, he always smiles, puts his thumb up and nods yes. I have no reason to feel that he is stressed or worried about it. I have spoken on several occasions to the Doctor, confirming that they are happy about things, and they say it will be good for him to have a break, so I am going with their blessings.

I bought him an advent Calendar, and he is counting the days off, he never forgets to open the window for the chocolate every morning as I arrive. I also bought a small Xmas tree plant from the supermarket for his room, when I saw it it made me smile, and I knew it would make Gary smile also.

I know that some people have reservations about us doing this trip, people keep saying, "Oh it's a long way", or "do you think it's safe?" It is a three-hour drive, that is nothing for me, and I am used to driving in the snow. We will have a stop off half-way for coffee and to stretch our legs, it will be very pleasant. But I think it is important that he sees and understands that I am not afraid to take him away from the clinic, and that I am not worried about him, I'm sure it will make him feel more confident. If he thought I was afraid, then he in return would feel fear for himself, once fear sets in, it would be very difficult to eradicate it, then normal life would be harder to maintain.

CHAPTER THIRTEEN

It is during the worst storms of your life,
that you will get to see the true colours,
of the people who say they care.
Some you will expect,
others will surprise,
and some may disappoint.

There is such a festive atmosphere around the clinic, but this by no means impacts on therapy classes. His classes have increased on a daily basis, and he copes really well, and seems to enjoy them. He is very enthusiastic about each class and I attend them with him, this gives me the best opportunity of understanding what is going on and also on progress.

If I know what the therapy involves, then I can get him to practice it every-day, there is a lot of spare time during the day, and he would soon get bored just sitting around, that would definitely not suit him. I am certain that the extra therapy during each day is paying off and moving him forward quicker.

My presence is accepted happily by the majority of the staff, but for sure there are one or maybe two, who, let's say, don't seem convinced, but I know my husband better than they do, and I am not here to win any 'Miss Popularity Contests', if they don't like it, then it's their problem not mine.

Gary has my enthusiasm to pull on, I watch and see how many others, just take to their room when they are between therapy, there are also patients who don't attend all of their sessions during the day. I find it very odd and also disrespectful, that some people just refuse to attend. Everything here is about their recovery, if you don't take this opportunity in the early stages, then your recovery will suffer greatly. Of course, there are also the other type of people who, like Gary are hungry for recovery, people who can self-motivate themselves, I have the greatest respect for these individuals

My main concern has always been, the language barrier for Gary, I know he would feel isolated much of the time, and he gets bored very quickly, like most people he would then spend too much time on his own in his room, this would be very emotionally draining for him.

It is very important that I infuse fun and laughter into our day, for instance, when we go to the Gym, we both use the bikes, we face each other and we cycle to imaginary places, I talk about the scenery, and how far we will travel, and I sing a special song when he starts to get tired. *(the original words were written by Charlie Chaplin)*

Smile though your legs are aching,
Smile though you feel their breaking,
Smile though a tear maybe ever so near.
If you feel blue,
I'll make the sun shine through.
Then that's the time you must keep on peddling,
Although you may think I'm meddling,
If you smile, then you'll get by.

This has become our theme song every afternoon, it makes everyone smile, and puts that wonderful sparkle into Gary's eyes, it makes us laugh on our imaginary bicycle journey around Switzerland. I look out the window and describe the imaginary blue lakes that we are passing, and the snow-capped mountains, profiled against a deep blue sky with the sun warming our faces, the occasional Falcon soaring high above us, as we head for a Cappuccino and Apple Strudel, or setting the scene of following the winding Spanish coastline, with the crests of waves lapping at the shore, reminding him of the feel of sand between our toes when we walk along the beach, the hot Spanish sun tanning our arms and legs, looking forward to a glass of wine and Tapas at the end of our ride.

Everyday I narrate a different journey, a different Country a different place in time, we easily get lost in our amazing journeys, struggling to peddle up steep hills, and coasting down the other side with the wind blowing our hair, waving and saying 'Hello' to people passing by in the corridor, as if they are part of our story.

We laugh so much, and occasionally we even shed a tear as my descriptions sometimes mirror actual journeys that we have taken on our motorbikes, but that is ok, our emotions are not for hiding right now, we need to feel, we need to hurt to enable us to heal.

Instead of Gym therapy being a chore, especially as Gary was never a Gym type of person, our Gym experiences are always fun, and we bring that fun to people around us, shouldn't it be a great feeling to know that you made someone smile, someone who was possibly at one of the lowest points in their life? The people around us can enhance or detract from our day, far better to make some-one's day better.

By now Gary is very popular with both patients and staff, he has that winning smile and that generous personality that draws people in, his lack of speech, does not deter him now, on the contrary, it's actually easier for him I think, because he can't speak, he has alternative ways of communicating, and therefore does not have to worry about the language barrier, whereas, it is harder for me to communicate when people try to chat to me in German.

It occurs to me, that because everyone is aware of Gary's speech loss, they are prepared for it, so there are no expectations of him, also the staff are used to it in the clinic, Gary is not the first person they have encountered with speech loss of course. Whereas I am afforded little excuse for not speaking German, everyone assumes that because Gary has lived here for six years, that I also must have been here with him full time. So, you see, I am very disadvantaged on a different level.

In every situation in life, even in this one, there are times when the partner of a stroke survivor will feel that she or he is having a hard time, I often feel it, like dealing with his financial affairs or worrying about when the car needs a service, trying to sort out my residency, to name but a few, and when I start to feel hard done by or stressed, I have to sit myself down, give myself a good talking to and say to myself. "In the grand scale of life, how important will this problem be in a year time?" The answer to myself, "Not at all".

One way or another, like it or not, a problem will be sorted, no problem goes on forever, so I can at least smile to myself and hope that I get it sorted sooner rather than later, and I have learnt, through this experience, to enlist people who know more about the problem to help you, don't be too proud to ask. I say to people all the time, my stress is always about official stuff, it is never about Gary, he is my pleasure never my stress.

Gary has proved himself to be the man I married, I have never doubted that, he is still the man I've always known he was, but now he is my Hero in every sense of the word. Where other people may crumble and complain, he stands tall and fights to conquer.

Gary takes advice, he never takes anything as criticism, this is part of why he does so well, he trusts that I know best at the moment, and he is happy to take my lead. Some people can't be told, some people don't listen, lots of people are so caught up in tragedy and what they have lost, that they can't see that they have so much still to build on. Gary can see that things have changed, and may never go back to how they were, but he also accepts that I will make his life the best life we can have together. It's how we manage the future with what we can do, not with what we can't do.

Our life now is not about mourning what we were planning to maybe do in the future, that he thinks we can't do now, it is more about moulding the world around us to fit in with us. We will never subscribe to giving in to what other people's expectations are for us, we will always make our own route.

When a doctor said to me at the beginning of our journey, that Gary may not walk again, my response was. "that will never happen on my shift". Well we have already proved that point, and Gary is strong and healthy, he is determined and trusts in me, this is still the beginning and we have proved so much to each other, that we have no doubts dragging us down. Don't succumb to people telling you what you can't do, only dream of the things you think you can do, and they will be your reality

CHAPTER FOURTEEN

DEFINE THE WORD HERO

A person who is admired for their distinguished courage, outstanding ability and achievements, of noble qualities. Someone who puts others first in difficult situations.

I see pain and anguish during some therapies, I see his struggles, I see his frustrations both inwardly and outwardly. What I never see is a lack of desire to conquer. His will is strong, his need is greater, and his desire for recovery his biggest ally. I am just his Mentor for now, and he looks to me for that leadership and I am obtaining the tools to teach him further.

My understanding of the injury that this type of stroke causes is becoming clearer. I by no means consider myself an expert, but I ask a lot of questions and I have done a lot of research online, of course, I do not know the workings of what happened, and truthfully, it does not matter who I ask the question "why did this happen? No one can give me the answer, I am certain that this will be a source of frustration to me forever, I am the sort of person who needs answers, but for now I have to accept that the answer is no answer. As I am Gary's voice for now, I think the experts find it a little difficult to deal with it. I don't think they are used to being asked questions they can't answer, but hey ho, I will continue to ask if I feel the need to.

Gary's long-term memory is returning slowly, I think this will be a natural thing rather than a processed one. He has started to remember people now, if I show him pictures of friends, he knows them but cannot, as yet remember their names, when I tell him he recognises the connection, but if I show him again half an hour later he can't remember again, so his short-term memory is still a big problem. It's not the remembering people that is distressing, it's learning a word then forgetting it almost immediately. I tell him my name, and he is so happy when he says it, but he won't remember it seconds later unless I tell him again.

Speech and memory are the slowest to come back. if he learns to walk up the stairs, he won't forget that, and with practice he will get better and better, that's the difference with the physical side of things. Patience is the best thing you can practice with the speech and memory. Every day, I practice recall with him, whether its people or objects. He still can't identify his own body parts, but I am now making visual thoughts for him, for instance, I point to his nose and ask him what it is, he will shake his head, so then I say " it's nose," he will then repeat nose, I then say, " Nose, keep it out" and he will repeat it. I talk to him about being nosy, when he is looking at something, I say nose many times a day, after a while, he could touch his nose and say it on his own, it's kind of like word association I suppose, but it works for him.

When we go for our daily walks outside, I ask him what things are called, trees, steps, flowers, cars etc etc. If he can't say it, I tell him and he repeats it, it may take some time, a week or maybe more, but eventually he will remember it. Repetition is the most important thing for recovery, the brain has to accept things back that it does not automatically know any more.

He is doing well with his arm function, but has to be reminded all the time, if his arm is hanging down by his chair, he will not feel it, his brain has lost his right arm for now, I have to constantly tell him to put the arm in his lap, it's very bad for it to be just hanging motionless. He has no sensory at all in arm or hand, he can't feel pain in it, heat or cold, and of course this can be dangerous. I have tried ice and heat and he can't feel either. So, this is something I intend to work on. Without any feeling in his fingers it would be very hard for him to learn to pick anything up. After researching this subject I am very confident that we can return the feeling for him.

Today, he had his eye test, if you remember, Gary had no peripheral vision, he had to turn his head completely to look to the side. I have been fully aware of this, and if I waved my hand at the side of his head he didn't know, but over the weeks, I have been convinced that this is improving. Well today proved me right, his eye-test shows his peripheral vision is back. This is such an important result, it's going to help his balance amongst other things, so today we have great cause for celebration, it calls for an Apple-juice at dinner.

Strokes of course leave a multitube of disadvantage, some we will overcome, others we may not, but looking at things as a whole, there are also temporary advantages, coping mechanisms I like to think of them as, and it is important to see these as early as possible, for example, his short term memory loss, if I tell him something, or teach him something, which he forgets later, he doesn't have any fears about it, or worry about it as he is unaware that he has forgotten.

A lot of what is going on in Gary's brain protects him from stress and harmful emotions, for now he doesn't really miss too much of his life as he doesn't remember it. I miss our home in Spain, whereas he doesn't remember we have one. I like to think of it as the brains way of protecting him for now. He is on anti-depressants, which is normal for stroke survivors, so there is also a manufactured aid in place, for this I am very grateful, but also know that at some point he will have to come off them, but hopefully we will be steadily progressing in a positive way through our journey.

We play cards, I have to prompt him all the time, but over a period he is getting better and he is remembering so much easier, again, this is a form of memory practice we do every evening.

Gary's brain is like a sponge, soaked in water, unable to absorb but a few drops at a time, his brain is full of knowledge, the knowledge of a lifetime, he doesn't need to absorb more, the knowledge has to be unravelled and then he will start to process it properly again.

He is blissfully unaware of the simple tasks he now finds momentous, but tries every day fearlessly to conquer, day after day, we repeat the same tasks repetitively, and he looks to the tasks with enthusiasm, and a hunger for learning, I am always in awe at his tenacity and desire to succeed in such difficult circumstances, with once, simple tasks. I know he will always be the tool I use to keep going on this journey.

It is not just my strength that drives us forward, no of course not, it is his strength of character that feeds my ego and desire, for the view that awaits us at the finishing line.

I have become one of the cogs in this wheel, integrated in the machinery that drives hope along the tracks.

I am so grateful and appreciative of being allowed to be a part of this, and I don't just mean to the Clinic or staff, I am so grateful and humbled that I am in the position to give up my life for now to support Gary totally, I have worked hard all of my life to be financially secure, now I know that there was a reason for it above my own ambitions and plans..

This is a warm friendly environment, where people are treated with respect and compassion, where support is given freely, it is a bubble, a cocoon of safety for us both for however long we need it. I will forever be indebted to Switzerland for their system of humanity and caring.

Every day these experts build his hopes and confidence, I build his plans and dreams. Together I think we are a formidable team all supporting each other on a tricky, sometimes steep climb, but whenever we look down, we don't see the drop, we just see someone holding tight to our ropes.

Gary is never afraid to ask me for help, he knows I am always there, and nothing will change that.

CHAPTER FIFTEEN

Every morning I drive to the clinic.
I have joy in my heart,
And faith in my soul.
His smile is a gift to me

The time has passed quickly from conception of the Xmas in St Anton idea and the reality of the journey. We are both so excited about having Xmas together, away from the sterile World we live in now, looking forward to restaurants, bars, snow, Xmas trees and fairy lights, who could blame us?

As people start to find out about my plan to drive the three hours to Austria and spend Xmas Eve there, then return for seven o'clock Xmas night to the clinic, I sense some have reservations. It's a long way they say, some say nothing which means so much more, I understand they are nervous, mostly for Gary, but I have thought this through very thoroughly, and it's the correct thing for us.

It's just over seven weeks since the stroke, and I am sure that the majority of people in our situation would be swept along with the clinic Xmas itinerary, only there is no real Xmas itinerary! There will be a skeleton staff, people who are able will return to their families for two days. If we spend the time at the apartment, we will have little Xmas cheer, no friends or family visiting, no Xmas tree, a solitary lunch together which I have no desire to cook.

St Anton will bring happiness, we have memories there and I am sure the Hotel staff will welcome us warmly, pre-stroke I know Gary would have loved the idea of this jaunt, and this person is still there, his character has not changed, part of it is just locked away at the moment, but this does not mean that I don't remember who he is, it is for me to help him to return to himself fully.

His long-term memory loss, I am sure, is helped by recall. I show him a photograph of someone, or some place, there is no recognition, just a complete blank. If it's a friend, I will tell him of things we did together, where they live how long we have known them etc, he takes time to process the information. I repeat a lot of the information, adding more details, I look into his eyes as he tries to connect the picture with the information, it is so strange to watch.

He is unblinking for an unnatural amount of time, he breathes shallow, it's like he is motionless in this time, he is sorting through a foggy maze in his head to find the connection, nothing else exists for these minutes, his brow is not furrowed, he is not stressed, he is just deep within himself, he is far away, somewhere I cannot go, searching, searching, it's like looking for a particular book in a library where a thousand books have fallen from the shelves to the floor, and you know it is there somewhere but where do you start.

He searches for a while, then just like he has found that buried book, he finds the person, it's that lightbulb switching on moment we have all experienced at least once in life, he smiles delightedly and says "Yes".

I am confident, that being in St Anton will be a great way of jogging his memory, actual places he loves and people he knows, the more we can open that memory up the better he will move forward with healing his Aphasia. He needs long term memory to remember things and short term to hold on to them.

The Aphasia stops him from recognising pictures of objects, but the actual object in front of him he will know. For instance, if I ask him to point to a picture of an Elephant, he does not know which it is, but if an Elephant were in front of him, he would know. He does not know a picture of keys, but if I ask him to give me the keys from the table he can. For sure, it could be very dangerous for him to be internet shopping for a gift for me, how the prospect of that one made us all laugh.

Gary still struggles with his urinary infection, caused through the stroke, it's very common and we have been told it could take a couple of years to clear, or may even leave lasting problems, it can sometimes occur during the night when he is unable to reach the bathroom on time, so, we are packed off with necessary pads and sheet protectors for the overnight stay.

This particular problem is a source of upset for him, but that is to be expected, I never make a big deal of it, and I assure him always, that this will get better in time, but never the less it would be upsetting for any of us. I always have to be aware of this when we are out and about, checking often whether he needs to go. In itself this is a delicate area, he is an intelligent human being and I don't want to make him feel like a child, so generally, when we are out, I tell him I am going to the bathroom and he should go too, quick statement and done.

It is never hard work, it's just a jaunt really, we love working together, we are both enthusiastic every day, it has made us both very strong.

His pain is my pain, his strength is my strength, his triumphs are also my triumphs, there is no failure.

I left him tonight, in bed, watching football on his iPad. His team Liverpool. He can now remember his password, to open his iPad, he can find You Tube, this is another positive step, he struggles to key in words, so we will do more work with this.

The Stroke

Every day we spend together, it's almost like nothing is wrong, like we are part of a project, or a reality show. "The Stroke" does not seem important here, we don't talk about it, it doesn't matter in this safe house, then suddenly Gary will be unable to perform what was once a simple task, or cannot remember something I told him seconds ago, and I am reminded why we are here, but even during these times I never feel dread or sadness. I almost just see an innocence, a naivety that I knew he possessed, but it wasn't so near to the surface, like it is now. The innocence we all have, but is buried in adulthood, forgotten or not suitable for show in our everyday lives. The necessity of growing up takes our innocence away.

All the stresses and strains that we have to deal with every single day in our normal lives, have just melted away, I don't discuss with him much of what is going on outside of the clinic, I have to deal with the officialdom and legal matters, he can't do anything to help so no point in involving him, but I envy the way he can just live in the moment, it's like he has no desire to bother about anything outside of his structured life.

I am happy that whatever coping mechanism that kicks in, helps him to cast off fear and dread, how much worse it would be for both of us if he was also stressing and worrying about everything. I have enough of that to deal with myself.

Tomorrow he will have assessments, these of course will form the final go ahead for going away overnight, I don't feel concerned at all. We are confident and feel strong and ready for our trip.

Today I received a text message from Gary's colleague, Vitali, you may remember he came to visit Gary in the Hospital and was a great help to me when we transferred to the Clinic, he asked if he could pop to the flat this evening. I was a little surprised but said 'yes of course'.

What a thoughtful and wonderful surprise, Vitali had picked a small Xmas tree out complete with lights and baubles. The tree was a fresh one, the baubles shiny and bright red, full of Xmas cheer and happiness, I am so overcome and have difficulty keeping my emotions in check. That he would think to bring this cheer to the flat and my solitary World, will be something I will never forget, this gesture meant so much to me, I couldn't wait to tell Gary, and it has a well-deserved place in this book.

I felt such joy when I trimmed the tree, I gave it pride of place on the table, the lights catching my eyes and making my heart smile. I am sure I did not convey just what a humbling experience this was and how energising the gesture was, from this almost stranger, but it was a huge form of pleasure for me, truly bringing Xmas into our home.

This morning the Doctor checked in on me whilst Gary was having his afternoon nap. She asked how I felt in myself, how I felt inside, she said she knew I was always smiling and laughing, and helping out with other patients, but was I looking after myself.

She offered me an appointment with the psychotherapist if I would like to talk to someone.

I replied that I felt happy, content, I never had dark moods or doubts about the future. Gary is doing well, and I was very confident and hopeful for the future. I told her that I relaxed in the evenings and spoke with friends by video call, and I didn't feel anxious about anything to do with Gary. She said, "Well could you tell us your secret!" we both smiled at her joke.

I thought about this for a few moments, and I replied, I didn't ever feel that this would greatly change our life together but did know already that it would enhance our feelings for each other and our future together.

I feel lucky that Gary trusts my every decision to direct him down the best path to our journeys end, he has so much faith in my ability to deal with things, as I have in his ability to cope.

I have never been afraid to face demons that enter my life, I am not about to start now. I will stand and face any demons that dare to cross me, just as I have in the past, and I will be the stronger. Never let those demons into your soul, they will dissolve your strength and strengthen your fears.

Define Demon: An evil spirit or Devil, especially one thought to possess a person or act as a tormentor.

For now, there is peace and a glass of chilled white wine waiting for me back at the apartment, tomorrow will be busy and bustling with our team, and full of excitement and anticipation for the festive season.

CHAPTER SIXTEEN

You think you have all the skills you need,
to complete your life plan,
then suddenly, you are on a new journey.
Learning new skills.
Skills that will enable you,
to carry on being the people you are,
enjoying the life, you have mapped out.

Today I am so excited, our last day before Xmas and when St Anton bewitches us with its joy and hope, its revelry and atmosphere. Knowing that everyone will be in a happy place and we will be part of this place. Leaving the clinic behind for a short while and re-joining a World that we know so well and a place we are so familiar with.

It will, of course, be bitter-sweet also, facing our fears of having to give up skiing, something we so love to do, but as I keep telling Gary, no one knows what another year of recovery can bring, never say never I tell him. Nonetheless, I am fully aware that it may cause a little sadness even heartache, but sometimes reality has to be faced, I have faced it and I am ready to help Gary face it.

Things have to be faced as they arise or as is necessary, I am fully aware at this point, that many of his hobbies and everyday activities are impossible, I am also convinced that many will be achievable again over time. Unfortunately, I do not know when or which, but maybe that is a good thing.

Would it be better to accept now that you will never do something again? Give up all hope of recovering a skill? I don't believe so, I feel it is far better to hold on to that hope and then you are far more driven to keep trying. I will always encourage Gary to believe even in the impossible because I believe in it, we have already broken through barriers we were virtually told were impossible, what may seem to other stroke survivors as too hard to attempt, I will never let Gary have that feeling. I will be his mentor, I will fill him with confidence, if he falls, I will swoop him up in my arms of encouragement, if he feels tired, of trying I will energise him with my enthusiasm, if he feels low, I will lift him with my spirit of adventure.

Nothing is impossible, just impossible to see sometimes, I have always been able to see beyond impossible, I can give Gary this gift so he can see beyond also.

We have no time for the 'why's and what-fore's' yes sometimes I get a little angry inside when I am forced to question the reason "Why", but I am only angry for Gary. I am first to understand, there is no authority or body to ask, not even a higher one, there will be no answer, so I am also quick to dismiss such absurdity, to ask a question that there is no answer to is beyond stupidity, far better to be asking for useful information that will have positive answers.

I do have some reservations sometimes, that when his safety net of memory loss, is no longer there, that he may get angry with life, frustrated with the place he is in, but I will be strong enough to steady him, and that this book will show him where he started his journey and how far he has come. He will see how strong we have been and how steadfastly we trudged through some of the darkest days of our life, towards the light shining ahead for us.

He will know that he has been as much my strength as I am his, he will learn about his own character, his own strength and resilience, he will realise that his willingness to allow me to lead him, has made me stronger and more determined.

We may never leave this journey's path completely, but we will go back to our life, and be ever grateful for reaching the summit.

We are together ten hours a day, we are happy together in every sense of the word, our respect and love for each other is palpable, it could never be more than it is now or in the future.

This is our here and now, nothing else matters outside of this World, his recovery is the only important thing. If he wants to shut everyone else out, then that is how it has to be, he just does not want to deal with anyone, friends or family.

I know it is terribly hard for his parents, they are so far away, I agonise and struggle every day over whether to just let them visit, but worry about going against his wishes, I feel for them, but they just have to be patient, the time will come when he feels confident and then they will return to our fold. Stress is definitely not a good thing for his brain as it is in the healing process and I cannot jeopardise his trust in me.

I am aware that they may be thinking it is of my doing, that I am preventing them from coming to see him, but again, the future will hold the answers for them, and everything will turn around.

What a busy day today, lots of work for Gary, each therapy carries an assessment today, and watching I feel very pleased, and he is very upbeat in his mood, his therapists are all happy with his progress and "amazing" seems to be the word of the day.

Physically he is showing great progress and we receive lots of praise for our commitment and tenacity. His Aphasia is still a major problem for his recovery, speech being very slow to come back, his memory however seems to be slowly but surely returning so I hope that will help with his learning process.

He is definitely communicating better, and a little more confidently, he knows everyone here now and they are our friends and family for this period of our lives, so he is not embarrassed or awkward in their company, and of course everyone else has similar problems.

It is a different matter when he is out and about near strangers, he can become very withdrawn and reliant on me, but wouldn't we all be the same?

Every day here at the clinic, I am witness to all these people who have the same struggles as Gary, some more severe, some less, I see someone who has severe facial paralysis struggling to smile at me, but I see the smile in her eyes, many people who have severe speech loss, but still able to communicate with us. Their struggle to exist beyond their stroke is fearsome, just as Gary's is, they want to be seen as the person they were before, it's something I can feel.

We know that strength is physical, but without the strength coming from your inner being and your mind, it will not be strong enough. It takes immense inner strength to smile when things are not going as you expected, or maybe hoped for, but a smile to someone else can mean reassurance, give hope to carry on. Let a smile be open to anyone else who may need one, whether you know them or not. A smile to a stranger maybe the thing which brightens a troubled mind or makes a day more bearable.

Gary has his cute crooked smile ready and available for everyone, he is enough to cheer anyone's mood, but then he always was a cheerful character with a ready smile.

Everyone is extremely happy with the progress he has achieved, and we have the blessings and good wishes from everyone here for our Xmas trip.

Gary is exhausted after his busy day so I decide he should have an earlier night and I will be able to get the car packed up and have a relaxed evening myself.

I spend a little time reassuring him about the journey, he still asks me where we are going, and I have to remind him it is Xmas Eve tomorrow and we are going to St Anton. I am very used to the look of confusion on his face when he thinks I am telling him something for the first time, but he responds with a smile when I show him his advent calendar with just 2 doors to open. I have written down for him that I will be here at 08.00 p.m. and I have left his clothes out on the chair, otherwise he would just put his track suit on as normal, these are the things he struggles to remember, anything out of his daily routine is too difficult.

I leave him comfortable and relaxed in bed with his iPad and I know he will be asleep very soon.

On my drive back home, my thoughts start to drift, I feel a little sad that I am spending this evening, at this festive time, alone in Switzerland, no pre Xmas drinks or Salon Party, no distributing gifts festively wrapped, no anticipation of opening gifts under the tree on Xmas day.

The reality soon comes into my mind, I am going to St Anton with Gary, and I know how different that could have been, my Xmas gift is that I still have him here, I could be spending Xmas day without him, this soon makes my mood happy again, and I think about the many people, too many, who will spend a lonely Xmas without a loved one. I am grateful for this night.

I will speak to family and friends and let myself get caught up in their festive plans but will also enjoy chatting about our plans.

Xmas, like everything else in life, is what you make it, and I have a feeling ours will be in the good memory chest for a great time, not in the bad memory chest for the worst Xmas ever.

I have wrapped the few gifts I have for Gary and I have packed two dresses I bought on the internet, everything is in the car, and I am ready for the road trip, organised like military precision.

CHAPTER SEVENTEEN

There is a time when you think you have it all
Then fate gives you your all
It's then that you realise the all
Is what you have at any moment in your life
I am happy with my all
for now
Be happy with your all

I arrive at 07.55, looking forward to seeing Gary's smile, and expecting that maybe he will be confused about our plans again. But to my surprise he is sitting in the reception lounge, he looks so handsome and just his old self, a nurse is chatting to him, they spot me, and both smile widely at me.

The nurse tells me that they have been talking about our Xmas plans and that she wishes us a safe journey and a very Happy festive season, I thank her and wish her the same.

Our trip begins here, once we are in the car, I go to set the satellite navigation, as my directional skills are nil, and I really mean nil. I could get lost in my own front room if I changed the furniture around, Geography was my worse subject at school, I found it boring and rarely listened or participated, hence my lack of geographical knowledge, and understanding.

It takes me approximately five successful trips to even the nearest place, to be able to do it from memory, so somewhere 3 hours away would be impossible without help. Sat Nav is my best friend; however, Gary was the opposite, he was brilliant, but I am very surprised when he shook his hand at me, intimating that I did not need it! Ok, this is a surprise to me, so I say to him. "You don't want me to use the Sat Nav?" "No" he replies. I have to admit I am both surprised and a little apprehensive, it's a complicated journey for me at the best of times.

My amazing husband never misses a beat or a turn, he is on the ball every step of the way. We even stop at our favourite Services for breakfast, I have actually missed this turn twice with navigation!

Gary goes to the toilet which is downstairs, he insists on going alone, I watch him and I am reminded of his struggles and his resilience, he is such easy company, as he always has been. No tears and tantrums, no self-pity or recrimination, he does everything for our future, never just for himself.

In the few moments sitting there alone, I think how amazing it is that I can adapt and settle into such a strange world and life, it really shows me how adaptable we can be if we stay focused and live in the here and now.

For example, we have done this trip many times, the format is the same, but the essential part will be missing, the skiing. We could have stayed at home and not come, but what would that achieve?

Making this journey for me is a test of our character, we can enjoy everything as we always did, and not mourn the skiing, leave that to one side this time, but we will not discard it completely.

I have told Gary that no-one knows in the future whether he will ski or not, I have reminded him that we have seen people with one arm or prosthetic leg skiing, amazing blind people skiing, I have always been in awe of these incredibly brave and adventurous human beings, so who is to say he won't be a member of this club of courage.

This trip will be about Xmas, enjoying nice food and revelling in the atmosphere. This time of year, the skiing is always secondary, we will be amongst happy people and enjoying a freedom away from the clinic, I will not let him mourn his skiing, no, I will enthuse him with hope for another time.

Our journey continues without fault, and I accept that the injury to Gary's brain did not affect his directional skills, this is a fantastic boost for him, he has taken charge, and control of our journey. And I am very relieved and happy that I can erase this from my job list.

We arrive at the Hotel door without incident, I am so happy for him. There is a very warm welcome for us, the owner is pleased to see us and deals with the situation perfectly, she warmly touches my arm and there is so much compassion in her eyes and in that small gesture that I feel the warmth through my whole being.

She insists we sit down and have a complimentary drink whilst the porter unloads the car and parks it. Such 5-star treatment, I can't say that I am not moved by it. I am however, a little unsure as to whether Gary remembers the Hotel or recognises the owner and staff but decide not to question him at this time.

Next, we walk across the road to the restaurant opposite, our favourite lunchtime eatery. The owner welcomes us with familiarity, but I see that look of surprise for an instant. It is fleeting and he recovers himself quickly and seats us.

I asked the Doctor at the clinic if Gary could have an alcoholic drink whilst we were away, she said yes, equal water to alcohol, so a glass of wine and a glass of water, that's no problem and we do not intend to be drinking much of course. So, I ask Gary what he would like, this will be his first alcoholic drink since his stroke, he points to a small beer on the next table and has that salacious look of expectation on his face, he always loved a small beer before a meal, a "Demi Pression" he used to call it from his time working in Toulouse in France. I order the beer and a white wine for myself, and we start to check the menu out, I look up to see Gary taking in the room, suddenly it occurs to me that maybe he does not remember being here, I ask him if he knows this restaurant and he says "No".

This comes as a real surprise to me, I had taken it for granted that he would remember, just then the drinks arrive, so the moment has passed for now. Gary hold his glass up and delights in looking at the cold beer, like it is the best drink ever, his smile says everything, he takes a sip, his face changes instantly to a grimace, like when a child tastes a lemon for the first time, he shakes his head and replaces it to the table, I say "don't you like it?" His reply "No". I started to laugh, and he followed suit, so now we know that his taste buds have also changed to a certain extent. I give him my glass and he tastes the wine and smiles broadly.

Every day is a learning curve for both of us, and it's amazing how one can adapt and settle into such an often strange World and environment, it really shows me how pliable we must be, if you are rigid in your life plans, then for sure you will never achieve them, there can be too many curve balls on the way. I decided very early in this journey, that as long as he is happily progressing it does not matter the time scale, and as long as I feel a sense of life going forward in a positive manner, then we are on the right track. My love for this man has proven to be immeasurable and knows no bounds, we are connected by an invisible force that only we can feel, it is tangible every day. We are acutely aware of each other's feelings, combined happiness is as important as our own.

If you don't have enough of a connection with that person, then your journey will be much harder, if you care about yourself first during this time then you will be unable to adjust. I know that if I can do the best for him, then it will ultimately be the best for me also. In this situation, it is so important to always remember that this was not his fault, no part of this is his doing, we have already been through this blame period, he blames himself because I can't ride my motorbike, or ski now. I have addressed this; it is not his fault he had a stroke and it is my decision not to do these things. He did not make those decisions, I alone made them. I am in control of the decisions I make, and I make them with him in mind of course, but they are made for what I feel is best. He owns no part of blame and he is reminded of this whenever I feel it is needed.

CHAPTER EIGHTEEN

Xmas brings happiness and sadness.
It depends where your life is at that point.
But I don't let life dictate to me.
I dictate how I feel.
Don't let anything lead your spirit.
Guide it yourself.

After lunch we wrapped up warm and cosy, fur lined coats and hats, snuggled in warm scarves, I love that feeling of being warm inside with cold noses and rosy cheeks, I have always loved the snow and especially walking in it, we leave the Hotel and I hold on to Gary's arm, slowly I say, and you will be fine, we have all afternoon, we can dawdle as much as we like, take in the atmosphere.

He seems very relaxed, maybe the glass of wine helps. We choose our path carefully and make our way through the village, lots of happy people milling around, some shopping for last minute gifts or maybe treating themselves as we usually would.

On route, I point to a bar "The Piccadilly", and ask him if he remembers it, he shakes his head, even though we have spent many a great evening in there, live music and dancing socialising with others for the evening. I remind him about the night he met the Irish guy who managed to make us laugh all night, I tell him how he made a new friend that night, spontaneously he says "Oh yes", and recognition comes on his face, he laughs out loud, he puts him thumb up, he now remembers.

Gary has a favourite bar in St Anton, both of us love it there, it's called Base Camp, I have mentioned it to him but he does not remember it, we are headed that way now, he has no idea where it is, so we just walk slowly enjoying the beautiful snowy Xmas scenery, lots of trees full of sparkling lights.

We leave the main road and have to cross the snow to reach the bar, I hold on tightly and coax him along, he is nervous but steady, as we turn the corner, he stops and smiles, nodding his head and saying "Yes", he remembers now, he can hear the music and that's the thing we love about this bar.

The bar is buzzing with people, the saxophonist is playing, the atmosphere draws us in, Gary is in one of his happy places again, we find a seat, I am so happy we came here. We enjoy the music as always, and partake in a little wine and water, we are happy to be part of this World, it may not be like before, but we are here, and Xmas has begun for us.

We leave after a couple of hours and stop on the way back to the Hotel for a hot chocolate, it's so warm in the coffee shop, our faces are glowing, and the hot chocolate is delicious. The smallest things can give such pleasure and we each know that our feelings are happy ones in this place.

We start our walk back to the Hotel again, unfortunately, maybe the cold outside contributed, but Gary got caught short, and couldn't get to a toilet fast enough, this sometimes happens still, and it never fails to make my heart ache for him. When it happens, I know it must hurt him deeply, but as always, he never makes a fuss, he deals with these things with patience and calm, but I know how he will be feeling inside. I too make no great response, just reassure him that it is temporary and will sort itself out soon enough.

For any adult, this type of thing has to be such a trial to them, the less fuss that is made the better, once he is in the shower I remove the trousers and underwear and place in a laundry bag I have brought with us, being prepared for every eventuality is the key to success. This incident will not be mentioned again.

I leave him to have a rest and I go down to the lobby where I bring my journal up to date and make my Facebook status for today, and of course I have a glass of wine, I have no driving for the first time since this happened and we are not going out tonight, so no fear of walking.

We have booked dinner in the restaurant here at the Hotel, as I didn't want to go out and I felt the atmosphere would be wonderful on Xmas Eve.

We both dress in our finery, well the best finery we could muster up in Switzerland, and I felt that we had scrubbed up well, and we go down to the bar.

The welcome that awaits us is unexpected, the owner and his wife are there and they invite us to join them for Champagne, they tell us how wonderful it is that we made the trip and they are honoured. Gary is overcome and his eyes glisten with tears, his emotions are so close to the surface at present, then we laugh knowingly at him and it passes.

The conversation flows, Gary is so intent on joining in, I have never seen him try so hard, he has spontaneous sentences, who knows how they come, but they are released from his memory, it's difficult to understand but who cares, it is wonderful to see. I see into the future of his speech recovery.

The Stroke

Dinner was wonderful, Gary does not like food which I have to cut up for him, I think this is one thing that reminds him of something precious that has been taken from him, he likes to pick food that he can eat with a fork, it's not always possible of course, but generally I can do it so fast that no one notices, tonight as we are having meat, I have asked the waiter if they can cut it up in the kitchen, they are happy to oblige so we have no tension or stress over this.

We are relaxed, there is nothing but cheer and happiness all around us and we are part of this scene, this will never be remembered as the worst Xmas, no it will have happy memories, I know my decision was the perfect one.

I wake early Xmas morning, as I do every morning, I have a lovely sense of excitement, I am looking forward to Gary opening his presents, just small gifts but all very meaningful. I gently wake him, as I don't want to waste a minute of this day, we have to return to the clinic by 19.00 hrs, so we must leave here at 15.00 at the latest.

From the smile that stretches across his face, he remembers that it is Xmas morning, we hug and I say 'I Love you' and he says I Love you back, I am always grateful that one of his first sentences was those three little words, it leaves such a warm glow inside me, and it shows every-time what a good heart he has.

Once we are showered and dressed, I give him his gifts, immediately he has a pained expression on his face, I knew he would be upset because he couldn't get me anything, so I quickly tell him I don't need anything this year, that my gift list only had him on it, and he is with me. Without him, what gifts would mean anything to me? So, we open the gifts, he cries. I shed a few tears, and we hug again, what more do we need?

We go downstairs to the bar, we had already decided we did not need breakfast before a festive lunch. We have one glass of Champagne, that's our quota for the day before my drive and his return to the clinic.

Whilst we are enjoying people watching and our Champagne, a group of carol singers arrive, perfect, you don't get that in your front room on Xmas day.

The owners wife arrives and comes to sit for a while, she asks Gary if he is having a good time he nods and says "I love you", I explain about his key words and sentences and she smiles and says "I love you too ", now starts the Love Bug that will continue throughout our journey, Gary makes everyone feel good, and everyone loves this response. It says so much about the person he is and about the big heart he has, many people have terrible key words and sentences, I hear them at the clinic, I am proud of the person that everyone can see in my husband, as always he is my Hero.

Lunch is soon over, and we ate too much, but that's what we do at Xmas, it is all too soon that we are packed up, the car is brought around, and we have to say our goodbyes. Everyone wishes us all the best and hopes that we will return again next-year, I know we both silently hope in our hearts the same thing.

It's time for us to return to the clinic and reality, but we have memories locked in our memory chests, Gary needs to make lots of new memories, that will replace ones that maybe have been erased, he seems very relaxed and content, and does not seem stressed about going back.

It's 18.30 when we pull into the clinic car park, the journey was clear all the way, not many people travelling on Xmas evening, we stopped once for coffee and made good time.

I happened to look up at the window on Gary's corridor, and there watching was his house master, he waved and moved to come and meet us.

He was due to go off shift at 19.00, so was very happy to see us, he asked about our trip and Gary's face was enough to say it all. We wished each other a Merry Xmas and it was time to call it a day.

Gary will be back to his full therapy routine tomorrow, so he needs an early night, it's been a busy two days for us, but very successful. I am proud of how we both handled what could be a very difficult time of the year.

CHAPTER NINETEEN

THE STROKE DID NOT OWN OUR XMAS

It's a strange world that we are living in now.
But it is a very safe and warm world for both of us.
One where we don't have to think about anyone else.
One where his recovery can take priority over everything.

Every-one in our lives has to take second place at present, including family, they are not a priority, we still need them on our side, but we can't give them Priority or VIP tickets to this show. We have to self-isolate and they have to understand without question.

I woke this morning feeling very positive and happy as always, but with a new feeling of successes coming our way.

I have many challenges myself to overcome, Switzerland is not an easy place when you are in this situation, there are many things to sort out, some proving more difficult than others. I have no status here, so I have no rights over Gary's affairs, this has to be tackled very soon, however, these matters are for another time, this book is about our personal journey, but there will be another time to address the ups and downs of not being prepared for the unexpected, and how we should all implement measures for the "Just in case"

After our post Xmas visit from the Doctor, we have great news, she feels that it would be a good thing for us to do things away from the clinic, providing it does not impact on his therapy time, so tomorrow we will go to the local supermarket for a small food shop for me and have a coffee there. Not exciting per say, but normality creeping in for certain.

Unfortunately I am unable to take him home yet as we have six flights of stairs and there is no lift, this is one of the immediately pending problems I face, looking for a new flat to move to, and I cannot say that it is something I am looking forward to, but face it I must so that we are ready for when Gary is discharged from this safe haven.

It is such a mixture of feelings and concerns for me, on the one hand I am desperate for him to be well enough to leave here, on the other I have reservations about how he will cope with just me to support him, I have no reservations about my enthusiasm to cope, but will this be enough?

I think about stuff all the time, like will he get frustrated when he can't make himself understood by others? When he feels tired quickly, when he has to adhere to food limits, it will be very different once we leave here, everything is in place to make life positive, everyone understands his needs, here he is one of many with the same problems, outside he will be one of few with little understanding.

I have to be his support and lead, I am lucky he has such a strong character, and a desire to conquer, I am lucky that he is doing this not just for himself but for me, he is not sorry for himself he is sorry for me, and this is a driving force like a hundred men charging forward. He wants this for me as much as himself, he is totally selfless in his fight to rule and conquer.

Sometimes he seems a little inward, distant, even sad, I know he tries to hide such feelings from me, but I see them like a mist curling around him, blurring his view, at these times I have to wrap him in my belief that the future, our future is still destined to be wonderful, we have a life still to plan, hopes and dreams to fulfil, I chat about the New Year coming, about how much we have achieved in just two months.

Every day we move forward inch by inch, sometimes there is a leap forward, maybe with his speech or his recognition skills.

Today, during our writing session together, he wrote the alphabet freestyle with his left hand, he has so far, been tracing over my writing. I have to say, in all honesty that it was beautiful, so clear and defined, much nicer actually than his original right-handed writing!

It may not seem like much to shout about, but he needs this skill to help him communicate, we have been working tirelessly, every-day practicing, and it has paid off, now we will form words, the first will be his name.

If I ask him what his name is, he does not know, neither does he know mine. When I say this, you need to understand a little more about the Aphasia, if I ask Gary to write his name or mine, he won't be able to, but if I call his name out, he will turn to look.

Inside his head, he can think about the question, and he can see the word "Gary", but he is prevented from communicating it to paper in word from or in speech form. Yet, if I gave him a song sheet to read, he could sing that song perfectly. This is because the speech is in a different area to the singing and has not been affected by the injury caused by the stroke.

To many people the speech will be the biggest challenge, and many partners will miss the communication between themselves, frustration on both parts is a difficult thing to overcome. I feel because we spend most of our waking time together that it is easier for us. Whatever he is trying to communicate to me will usually be about the here and now,

I don't need to ask him random questions about his day as I am present throughout.

It would be a lot harder if he spent his days at the clinic and I only visited him in the evenings for example. Then making conversation would be so much more difficult. Partners often feel they don't want to talk about their workday, or that they went for a coffee with a friend, or even convey feelings of happiness in their every-day life. Guilt is a trip that many people find themselves on. In reality, it is better to allow them to see that you are dealing with things well, your wellbeing is paramount to their success.

It's ok to feel that this has taken over your life to an extent, because that's the truth, but don't let it take over your relationship, it has no rights to that.

There will be times when you have to hand out tough love, this is a true test for you both, you will have to sit back and watch them struggle, turn a blind eye when they want your help, no matter how much it hurts, it is a necessary addition to any therapy success.

Now that writing has become an integral part of his communication, things are moving forward again, we set aside an hour every morning between therapy classes to practice. We sit at our little table in the corridor with our books and pass the time of day with the passers-by, other patients going to and from classes, nurses, cleaners and even visitors, it's a busy little thoroughfare, but most people by now are very familiar to us. German is the most spoken language of course and not too many people speak English, but with my rapidly improving German and Gary's thumbs up, we manage admirably. There are of course a few English-speaking people. All Gary's Doctors and therapist, do, of course, speak good English.

We often have visitors to our table to see how Gary is doing, or just to join us for a coffee and a chat, so you see how normality in any situation can be found.

Every evening after dinner we are back at our table to amuse ourselves and relax with a game of cards or dominoes or one of the many games, we have received from our wonderful friend Jackie, a constant support for our game cupboard.

This precious time is spent with laughter, relaxing in each other's easy company, discussing current affairs in England and bringing him up to date with my conversations with family and friends.

After being here for almost two months, I can't help but notice how, many people's visitors dwindle away. Friends come with enthusiasm in the beginning, but then they fall away fairly fast. People should try to put themselves in the same position and realise, visits from the outside are very important, there is a lot of down time here and, although much of it is often spent resting, I feel that everyone benefits from a visitor.

It is a huge undertaking for a partner to be the only visitor, many partners will work full time and then have to travel to the clinic, some may have children to care for. Life has to go on for them, so enlisting friends and family to visit on a regular basis can often be better than offering to look after the children. In this environment, every-day is virtually the same, so for those who have speech there is only therapy to talk about, for a partner to visit all the time, it imposes such limitations on conversation.

Gary and I are very self-contained, happy in each-others company, we have the same interests and hopes and dreams, our ambitions have always included each other, we are not really like two separate people anymore, this experience has drawn us into one entity, one life, almost one being, it sounds strange I suppose, as I have always been such an independent person, with a very big life of my own, but this seems right.

I don't talk of "Me" I talk now of "Us", and I am content with this. I have been alone many times in my life, have enjoyed selfishness and solitude at times, now I just want to be "Us".

Some-one asked me "How do you stay so positive?'

I replied, "I couldn't be bothered with the strain of negative"

The year is drawing to a close, a new year waiting to begin, we have been invited to our special friends Artur and Cristina's home here in Switzerland for New Year Eve. Gary has permission for an overnight stay at home and New Year's Day together.

When we are away from the clinic, I try to make things as normal as possible, our only difficulty are the stairs to the apartment, six flights and only a hand rail on one side, I have to support him and it is a slow journey, but we take it in our stride and we manage it well.

Once in his familiar surroundings of home, I allow him the privacy and freedom to do what he can, he attends to all his personal needs well, even adept at shaving with his left hand.

It can be difficult for me to watch him struggle, but if I feel he will be able to cope I let him, tough love is very hard to deal out but also very necessary for his continued recovery.

He appears very calm and tranquil, happy to be home. I wonder how he is feeling about seeing Artur and Cristina and their family, he seems at peace with it, I am hoping that this will open the door to him allowing his parents to visit and being comfortable around people he knows, but we will see.

I remind myself how different this could have been, with many other scenarios, our humour and good nature is carrying us through much of this tough journey. When I hear him laugh it reminds me that this stroke has not taken the person he is, away from me, it has instead, brought him closer to me.

It is soon time to leave for Artur's, and we are looking forward to it, but of course there is a certain amount of apprehension, they are not used to seeing him like this, I wonder how they will react to him.

My fears were unfounded, everyone was just happy to see us, on reflection maybe I was the most nervous, I have no real reason for this, it's just being in a different situation I suppose, but I soon relax.

It was such a lovely evening, great food and a glass of Prosecco to toast in the New Year.

Everyone was so easy and warm towards us, but I sense how hard it was for Gary, very little interaction, sometimes he looked bewildered, lost in his own place, it's so sad to see him so vulnerable, maybe it is too early for socialising with friends. He is comfortable with his surroundings at the clinic and the friends we have made there.

I decide that he needs more time and more speech, I sense that he will feel frustrated being unable to make himself understood, he needs to find a voice, and he needs to unlock more of his memory.

Amongst his strength there is a fragility about him that he has no control of, so many things he wants to do he can't, who could not understand that type of frustration, I have to steer him away from such negative thoughts, I have to clear a path of acceptance for this part of the climb.

I drive home, chattering about the evening, how nice it was and how nice to see everyone, he is very tired and quiet, but he so wanted to stay to see the New Year in, we did and now it's time for home.

Once we are in bed, he falls asleep immediately, I lay in thought, I have no feelings of reflecting on the past year for any bad reasons, under the circumstances, we had a good year with lots of lovely times and travel. I refuse to spoil the whole year for something out of our control that happened at the end of it.

Even in this situation, we still manage to have happiness in our hearts, me make life nice, not perfect but we don't mind, perfection is an impossible task to complete, and we don't do impossible.

I then start to reflect on friendships, who of my friends really has stepped up to the mark in our time of difficulty! It's often quite a revelation, to realise who wants to truly make a difference to your situation, not always the people you thought you could rely on, then again, others surprise you with their sincerity and kindness.

I think about new friends who have joined us on our journey, astounded by their kindness and support at unexpected times, small gestures that mean such a lot at this time.

My mind wanders to thoughts of social media, of which many people decry the power of Face Book. Without Facebook my journey would have been a lonelier one. Many have followed our journey, supporting us with compassion and humour, often on a daily basis, without this virtual contact, ties could have been lost to many friends.

Social Media played a large part in my ability to keep everyone updated with our progress, but also to allow them to see that we were coping and positively moving through our journey.

I believe that you should be kind to people just because you can, as you never know when you may need a little kindness back. Be good to people and you will get it back ten-fold, I believe that some of that kindness is being given back to us.

This experience may have distanced me from some friends but pulled me closer to others. It has promoted some acquaintances to friendships. I have felt the warmth from afar from people I hardly know, those who genuinely care with no benefit to themselves.

This New Year's Day, I am happy for myself, to understand that my marriage is filled with love and hope. Gary and I know we have it all within ourselves. We are strong and no matter where our journey ends, we will be together, holding hands, and we will always see the sun behind the clouds.

CHAPTER TWENTY

Love is a feeling.
Commitment is a decision.
We are all imperfect.
Love should be unconditional.
Without boundaries.

It is now exactly two months since "The Stroke", January 2nd 2019, it is also my Birthday, it has no consequence to me this year, and truthfully it is at an awkward time directly after Xmas and New Year, so I have never really celebrated it greatly for years.

At this time of year, we would normally go skiing for a week or maybe two, as skiing was a big part of our winter itinerary, especially since Gary moved to Switzerland. I need to address this and make sure he has peace with it, as I need to myself.

I know for certainty, he will mourn the loss of this great activity, he will certainly be sad for the fun times we had, and the people we met and interacted with, for the period of time, holiday friends, temporary friends, often remembered for their humorous input during Après Ski, numbers you exchanged, with promises to keep in touch, but of course rarely kept, with no malice on either side.

Of course we will both miss our skiing trips, it has been a big part of our lives, and it is distressing to think that again, the stroke has taken it away, sadness is but one of the emotions we feel, but I make him hold on to the belief, that he will one day again, be able to ski, I tell him he may never be "Frans Klammer", but he was never going to be anyway.

For me, I remind myself how many years I have been skiing, the wonderful times I have been blessed to enjoy, and maybe it is time I gave my body a rest from all that exercise, I am no spring chicken any more, and like lots of things in life, all good things must come to an end. If further recovery allows him to ski again then it will be a bonus for both of us. Till such time, we will pack our skis away, put this activity in a box, close the lid and lock it.

I will not mention my Birthday as Gary will not remember, he does not need a further guilt trip about presents and cards, after his sorrow at not being able to partake in exchanging gifts at Xmas. Being able to spend this time together is my gift, and the perfect one for me, I don't need "Things".

Is Gary holding on to his positivity? It's a question I don't have the answer to, maybe he is good at putting a brave face on, but I don't think that is possible in this situation, I do like to believe that I am succeeding in convincing him, with my never ending plans and positive chit chat. The most important daily outcome is, that he has faith in me, and that we can return, once again, to our life, and be happy, it is paramount that he can feel fulfilled and complete again.

It seems almost surreal today, that it has only been two months, 62 days, it has been a mammoth climb so far, but we have never faltered, I am proud of how we have held on to each other and found so much strength together.

I feel sometimes that life has sought to test me out, everything is done for a reason, I do believe this, sometimes the reason becomes clear, but often we don't get to understand it. However, I am finding it difficult to understand how life, could pick out a whole, perfect human being at random, and for no reason anyone can come up with, devastate that life, he is one of the sweetest men I have ever had the fortune to know. Where I am concerned, he opened his heart to me and allowed me to see into it, it is clear of anything other than goodness.

Yes, there have been times when I wanted to scream and shout, "This is not fair", but spending so much time at the clinic has taught me, that it isn't fair for anyone, and it isn't just a journey we are on. This happens to too many people, and it has no social barriers or age limits, it happened to my husband which means it can happen to anyone.

So many people are on the same journey, all have different battles to win, different obstacles to overcome, this book is dedicated first to Gary but also for all the brave people we have met along the way.

My hope is that my words can enthuse and even spur on someone when they feel life is too hard for them. To help partners to see a little clearer, and maybe help them to trudge a little easier up that next hill.

If you are just starting your journey, maybe this will help to see how far you can come in a short time, understand just how resilient we all can be.

Being a victim is not an option, that is the selfish way out, we must all be warriors, fighting whatever battle we are facing, it's not about he or me, it's about us, it's about sticking together. It's not just about "The Stroke", these rules apply to many situations in life. Times when we all may feel it's easier to give up. But those who fight on, succeed and get to stand at the summit and shout "We did it".

We have a long climb still to go, the summit is very high and distant, but it is in the sunshine, some days it may feel out of reach, but you just need to rest a while, there is no time limit put on our journey, we have many obstacles to overcome, but we know we can do it.

What we hope is that our supporters will continue our journey with us, embracing our successes and cheering us along our path. Remembering that we are still the same people and treat us as such please.

Gary just needs patience and respect. He loves you all, and needs your support as do I, life remains the greatest trip of all time, the alternative is unthinkable.

Sometimes reality can be too harsh,
And can slow you down.
Hopes and dreams are needed,
To sweep us further along our journey.
Impossible does not happen on my watch

Pauline Yates

Percychatteybooks
Story Telling (R)
Somerset House
6070 Birmingham Business Park
Birmingham
B37 7BF
Registered Number 2299335

Produced and published in the Hondon Valley, Southern Spain

Printed in Great Britain
by Amazon

49149638R00099